## *About the book*

THE UNDERGROUND MASS BOOK. For the first time, a book from—and for—the underground. A useful and revealing collection of prayers, songs and readings which have proved successful for underground groups across the country.

Here are nine experimental canons, most of them never before printed anywhere. Here, for today's youth and today's Christians, are more than 40 pages of readings from such traditional and contemperary authors as Hemingway, Berrigan, Lao Tzu, Merton, Hammarskjold, Simon & Garfunkel, Sartre, etc. Here, also, are 27 of the songs most often used by groups in all parts of the country.

This is what the underground is doing and where it is going. Complete with an introduction which puts the movement in focus and argues for an open and serious program of experimentation in the liturgy.

## *About the author*

STEPHEN W. MCNIERNEY, teacher, writer, journalist, and political analyst, is chairman of the Department of Philosophy at Loyola College, Baltimore, Maryland. He is a member of the Board of Directors and the Executive Committee of the National Liturgical Conference. He also serves as a member of the Baltimore Archdiocesan Liturgical Commission.

After study at the Gregorian in Rome, he received his M.A. in philosophy at the Catholic University of America and was a Fulbright scholar for two years at the Sorbonne in Paris, where he did extensive work with Gabriel Marcel. He is a frequent contributor to *The National Catholic Reporter* and travels extensively throughout the country lecturing on a variety of topics. His travels and associations have given him a wide knowledge of the use of the materials he has collected in this book.

# The Underground Mass Book

BY
STEPHEN W. McNIERNEY

Helicon • Baltimore

To
The Group in Baltimore
with special thanks to
Stephen J. McClure

Helicon Press, Inc.
1120 N. Calvert Street
Baltimore, Maryland 21202

Library of Congress Catalog Card Number 68-58310

# Contents

6

### THE SONGS

7

# Acknowledgments

The following authors and publishers have kindly allowed the use of selections from the works cited:

Ellen C. Masters: SPOON RIVER ANTHOLOGY by Edgar Lee Masters (Macmillan, 1914, 1915, 1942).

Lyle Stuart, Inc.: JOHNNY GOT HIS GUN by Dalton Trumbo.

Wesleyan University Press: AT THE SLACKENING OF THE TIDE by James Wright. Copyright © 1959 by James Wright. Reprinted from SAINT JUDAS by James Wright, by permission of Wesleyan University Press.

The Viking Press, Inc.: THE GRAPES OF WRATH by John Steinbeck. Copyright 1939, copyright © renewed 1967 by John Steinbeck. Reprinted by permission of The Viking Press, Inc.

Little, Brown and Company: ALL QUIET ON THE WESTERN FRONT by Erich Maria Remarque.

Paul R. Reynolds, Inc.: PRAGMATISM AND OTHER ESSAYS by William James, published by Washington Square Press, Inc.

Harper & Row, Publishers, Inc.: PROFILES IN COURAGE by John F. Kennedy; THE RELIGIOUS ASPECT OF PHILOSOPHY by Josiah Royce; GREAT SHORT WORKS OF STEPHEN CRANE by Stephen Crane.

Houghton Mifflin Company: THE COMPLETE WORKS OF RALPH WALDO EMERSON.

The Macmillan Company: *Man Is More* from ENCOUNTERS by Daniel Berrigan. All rights reserved. Reprinted by permission of the Publisher.

World Publishing Company: *The Face of Christ* from THE WORLD FOR WEDDING RING by Daniel Berrigan. Reprinted by permission of The World Publishing Company.

# Introduction

This book is frankly experimental. Nothing in it has been approved by those who have official charge of the liturgy of any church. Much of what it contains has not yet received the criticism and correction of those who are knowledgeable in liturgical, pastoral and theological matters. These prayers, songs and readings have been selected because they have proved successful for one group or another. The purpose of this book is to make these materials available to other groups across the country, so that what is good and serious in this collection may be improved, and what is ugly, trivial or purely local may be rejected. This is a book from—and for—the underground.

Some such book seems sorely needed. There have been a great many changes in the liturgy over the last five years, but little experimentation. The scholars charged with developing the new rites have been severely restricted in their efforts to test out their ideas through actual use in a variety of worshipping situations. They have had little freedom to adapt their efforts to the differing needs of different congregations, and thus no effective way to make sure that their proposals would effectively meet the changing liturgical needs of the post-conciliar Catholic.

Meanwhile the underground has proliferated. Small, informal groups all over the country have been trying to work out liturgical forms which would best express their life together as Christians. The efforts of such scattered groups, however, have been no substitute for a serious program of experimentation. Since church officials could not so much as admit of the existence of groups like these, the experience gained through private initiative was lost to the church as a whole. Most groups felt it necessary to maintain at least a semblance of secrecy, with the unfortunate result that there was no shared experience and one group could not profit from the mistakes and successes of others.

In this situation, perhaps this collection of materials used by various groups in different parts of the country will be of some value, both to other groups and to the church as a whole. But clearly, what is needed is an official program of experimentation. Merely testing prefabricated rites in certain selected "experimental" centers is not enough. In the first place, this procedure allows only for a selection among a limited number of predetermined patterns, all of which may be irrelevant; and in the second, the underground groups will not wait. These groups will simply go on developing liturgical forms which seem to meet their needs, and the split between the official liturgy of the church and that of some of its most dedicated and active members will continue to widen—perhaps beyond healing.

Genuine experimentation can end this split. Let the underground groups continue and redouble their efforts to work out more meaningful and appropriate liturgical forms, but let them also publish their results so that these may receive the criticism of those whose criticism is worthwhile. This will protect the underground against inbreeding and parochialism, which are death to the Christian spirit. It will also allow the official church to discover once again the voice of its people, without which the most solemn liturgical formulas remain dead letters in forgotten books.

Nothing should be approved merely because it is new, or because it happens to catch a momentary mood. Neither are things to be repressed merely because they are uncertain, unfamiliar or not to everyone's taste. The Christian people are not such children that they cannot tell the serious from the trivial, the beautiful from the banal, if given a chance. Those who feel the need and demonstrate the ability should be free to test what seems promising, to create, revise and adapt. But official approval should be reserved for those things which prove sound.

There is really no need to fear that the result of such experimentation would be chaos. The idea that any large number of congregations would immediately strike out on ill-conceived experiments of their own is really quite naive, as the experience of those churches in which there is freedom to experiment at the local level clearly shows. And the development of even the simplest liturgical form is extremely demanding creative work, as anyone who has attempted to design so much as a bible service can readily attest.

The dangers of a lack of experimentation, on the other hand, are quite real. A generation is growing up—one can meet them on any college campus and in most high schools—which feels itself deeply and thoroughly alienated from the official church and everything about it. These young people cannot understand why anyone should disapprove of their getting together to celebrate the kind of liturgy they find most effective, or why priests who join them should be persecuted. Consciously or unconsciously, they regard liturgical regulations as just one more example of the arbitrary imposition of the preferences of one generation on another. They are fond of pointing out that a group of folk singers or little children playing around an altar generates chancery outcries of irreverence, while a military color guard complete with trumpets and drums merits full-page coverage in the diocesan press.

Young people are not very good at rationalizations. They just do not take seriously those who tell them that liturgy must be the expression of the common life of the worshipping community, but that their own communities are to use only expressions which they find alien and artificial.

And so the young people are experimenting. Those who do not simply abandon the church will continue to experiment, whether the legitimacy of what they are doing is recognized by the official church or not. Because of this attitude, there has been a tendency within the official church to dismiss the young people in particular and the underground in general as an exercise in disobedience. Indeed, some church leaders have cited the development of underground liturgies as an indication that a generation of disobedient Catholics is emerging, led by disobedient priests.

This interpretation seems hopelessly wide of the mark. Liturgy is hardly to be construed as an act of loyalty toward a hierarchy. A group of Christians earnestly seeking to celebrate the life they share and seek in Christ can hardly be blamed if the words, gestures and songs they use differ markedly from those which seem most appropriate to bishops, who live every day surrounded by the formalities of the institutional church, or to scholars who are deeply immersed in the long tradition of developing liturgical forms.

Anyone who has taken part in underground celebrations in different parts of the country knows that these groups have almost nothing to do either with obedience or with disobedience. Few of them have ever heard of the central role which church documents and traditional theology assign the bishop within the liturgy of his diocese. Probably none of them has ever actually experienced a bishop fulfilling such a role. Neither the bishop nor his directives seem very real to such people, but their need for a meaningful liturgy does.

Restrictions and repression will not work in such a situation, no matter how high-sounding their justification. Authority means leadership, and the bishops cannot lead a movement whose very existence they officially ignore. Church leaders will have to admit that they have something to learn from these underground groups, and take practical steps to learn it, if they are to become once again effective teachers to the growing number of Catholics who are determined to have a more authentic and meaningful liturgy. For the sake of the whole church, it is time for the bishops to invite the underground to surface. It is time to invite and to encourage these groups to contribute what they can to the broad and varied program of continuing liturgical experimentation which is so vital to the church today.

The materials in this book do not by any means capture the variety and spontaneity which is to be found in the underground today. It is virtually impossible to indicate in print the range of options which the various groups have worked out, and which they employ according to the occasion, the mood and the circumstances. These selections are simply intended to indicate the kinds of prayers, readings and songs most underground groups seem to use in their eucharistic services. It should be clearly understood that no group would follow precisely the format indicated here, but that each would adapt these or similar materials to its own tastes and needs.

The underground abhors rubrics, and these have been entirely omitted from the Service section because each group works out its own. Some indication of the way in which the various prayers might be alternated between the leader and the group has been attempted by printing the leader's part flush to the left hand margin and indenting the parts which might be said by the entire group, but here also practice varies widely.

The canons printed here are the ones which seem to be used most widely, although at least two of them have never appeared in print before and are not generally available. A careful reading of these canons will reveal that they differ markedly in structure and tone, but it is still too early to tell which approaches are going to prove most satisfactory over the long run. A liturgist might remark that all of them seem to stress petition, rather than proclamation as might be more traditional, but again it is too early to tell how the different emphases will be adjusted in practice.

The readings have not been arranged thematically, even though many groups make a careful effort to develop a single theme in the readings and the discussion which follows them at any particular celebration. The readings included here are meant only to give some idea of the kind of things which some groups have found successful. The length of the excerpts printed here is also misleading, since some groups devote as much as an hour to hearing, discussing and responding to God's word before proceeding to the eucharistic meal.

The lyrics reprinted in the Songs section are probably the least representative part of the book. The musical tastes and abilities of the groups surveyed varied so widely and changed so often that it was impossible to give any reliable indication of what might be sung by any particular group on any particular day. The number of good, easy-to-sing songs suitable for celebrations of this type seems to be so limited that many groups prefer traditional songs, whether they are usually thought of as "religious" or not, and others prefer to use popular songs of the day, especially those of such groups as the Beatles, or of folk singers like Simon and Garfunkel. A number of groups have their own composers, who make up songs and teach them to fellow group members. At least to the untrained ear, some of these informal compositions seemed very effective, but most of them have never been transcribed in musical notation, and it would serve no purpose to print the lyrics alone.

The songs reprinted here do seem to be used very widely. Also, they are either so familiar that no group would require music in order to sing them, or they are songs for which the music is readily available in a songleader's book from one of the publishers who specializes in this area.

The order of service indicated in this book is merely suggested, and some comments drawn from discussions with various groups might be helpful. The "Call to Worship" is an extremely flexible and varied thing, sometimes rather lengthy while at other times merely a prelude to the readings which usually follow it. Of course, many groups begin their celebrations with a song; but other groups, particularly occasional groups, do not feel themselves in the mood or well enough acquainted at the beginning of their service for singing. The well-documented American reluctance to sing shows no signs of disappearing and many groups, particularly those which lack an effective song leader, find it wiser not to attack this reluctance at the very beginning of a service. Sometimes the call to worship is merely a few introductory remarks by the group leader, while at other times it consists in a short formula such as the one printed in this book.

Most groups turn immediately to three or four readings with a discussion homily and, less often, some sort of action in response to the readings. But other groups prefer to insert a penance rite, or rite of reconciliation, at this point. If the penance rite does occur before the main readings of the day, it is usually preceded by a short reading. If it comes after the readings, it is sometimes a part of the discussion homily, sometimes combined with the prayer of the faithful, or sometimes inserted after the prayer of the faithful as a reflection on how well the group has been living out the attitudes for which it has been petitioning. The rite of reconciliation printed in this book is merely an indication of a common form for such rites, and each group would add its own reflections to the three or four suggested.

Most groups seem to be omitting or greatly abbreviating the gloria. They seem to find it alien to an American way of speaking. The same thing is true, although less so, for the creed. Here the attitude seems to be that the responses to the readings and the whole eucharistic prayer itself are acts of faith, and that a special act of faith is better reserved to special occasions, such as a baptism. In this book, a simplified version of the gloria and of the creed are printed at the end of the service of the word as examples of what kind of adaptation is customary.

The prayer of the faithful usually follows the discussion homily. This is usually spontaneous and ordinarily the petitions arise immediately from the readings and the discussion. The form printed in this book is common, but once again group members would expand on the suggestions offered here with petitions of their own.

At the end of the service of the word, many groups pause for a song before beginning the eucharistic prayer. Most groups exchange some gesture of peace and friendship at this point.

Within the eucharistic prayer itself the variations which

are popular depend upon the particular canon which is being used. It should be noted, however, that a number of groups are beginning to develop acclamations, which they use after the words of institution and to conclude any canon they happen to be using. Two examples of such acclamations are printed at the conclusion of the first two canons contained in this book.

Concerning the meal itself, little generalization is possible except to say that this rite seems to be becoming shorter and more flexible. Most groups simply say the Our Father together and then communicate. With many groups there would be no blessing or dismissal except possibly at the end of the whole gathering. A concluding song, or even several songs, is common but not universal.

This book can give only a hint of the richness and spontaneity which exists today in the liturgies of the underground. It can give no hint at all of the reverence, the joy and the depth of Christian living which finds its inspiration and its expression in these gatherings. Perhaps this book will be of service to some of these groups. That would be good. Perhaps the materials collected here can even suggest some new possibilities to the church as a whole. That would be even better.

# THE SERVICE

# I. The Word

## CALL TO WORSHIP

Come, let us worship the Lord.
He is our God and we are his people.
> The Lord has called us together
> in peace, love and fellowship
> with each other and with all men.
> With joy and thanksgiving we celebrate
> the things the Lord has done for us
> and the great love he has for us.

## READINGS, RESPONSES AND DISCUSSION HOMILY

## PRAYER OF THE FAITHFUL

Father, you have spoken to us in your son and called us
together in your spirit. Listen to our prayers and help us
to do what must be done to mend our lives, heal our society
and build the community of your peace and love.

Lord, we ask for your peace, that we may turn from violence
and live the power of love.
> Lord hear our prayer.
Lord, we ask for your love, that we may get over our hatreds,
heal our divisions and work toward that unity
which is your promise.
> Lord hear our prayer.

Lord, we ask for your wisdom, that we may see the things that
have to be done, and find the ways to do them.

Lord hear our prayer.

Lord, we ask for your protection. Watch over this group,
our country, our church and our leaders.

Lord hear our prayer.

Lord, we ask for your kingdom. Strengthen our hope
in the new day of peace and love.

Lord hear our prayer.

\* \* \*

Father, hear and answer these prayers.

We turn to you in hope.

We ask you to lead us and to strengthen us
in your spirit.

Watch over us, our families, our country and our church.

Help us and our fellow Christians everywhere;
bring to all men the word of reconciliation,
justice, peace and love,
that is your son, Jesus Christ, our lord. Amen.

RITE OF RECONCILIATION

Let us confess our sins to each other and to God,
our merciful father.

Lord, we have remained cool to the fire of your word;
we have not dared to live for others.

Lord have mercy.

Lord, we have failed as your peacemakers;
we have continued to live by violence,
in our homes, our cities and our country.

Lord have mercy.

Lord, we have refused your freedom;
we have remained trapped within our narrow prejudices,
in the closed circles of the safe and the comfortable.
> Lord have mercy.
Lord, we have failed to love;
we have turned from those who love us,
and chosen not to see those who need us.
> Lord have mercy.

\*   \*   \*

Father, we confess and repent these and all the sins
> by which we have turned away from each other and from
>> you
> in our thinking, speaking and doing.
> We have done the evil you forbid,
> and have not done the good to which we are called.
> Our lives and our society are twisted, narrow and violent,
> and the guilt for this is ours.
> We do repent, and we are truly sorry for all our sins.
> Have mercy on us, kind Father,
> because of the obedience of our brother Jesus, your son.
> Forgive us all we have done, and not done,
> and help us to forgive one another.
> Confirm our repentance with the power of your spirit;
> move us now to live for each other and for you
> so that we may build a just and peaceful society
> and live the new life you offer us,
> through Jesus Christ, our Lord. Amen.
Our God is a loving father.
He forgives those who repent and turn to him.
May he forgive you your sins, strengthen your repentance,
and open to you the fullness of his life,
through Jesus Christ, our Lord.
> Amen.

GESTURE OF RECONCILIATION

*The following are sometimes used during the service of the word:*

## PRAYER OF PRAISE

Glory to God on high,
>    And on earth peace to men of good will.
>    We praise, bless, worship and glorify you.
>    We thank you for showing us your great glory.
>    Have mercy on us and receive our prayer.
>    Only you, Lord, are holy,
>    Only you are the Christ,
>    With the Holy Spirit in the glory of the Father. Amen.

## ACT OF FAITH

We believe in God,
>    father to all men,
>    who has called us all to work together
>    to build a new world of unity and peace.
>    We believe in Jesus Christ,
>    son of God and our brother,
>    who suffered, died and rose again for us,
>    that we might learn to live for others,
>    and find hope in his victory over death.
>    We believe in the spirit,
>    in the power of truth, of peace and of love.
>    We believe in the church,
>    the unity and fellowship to which all men are called,
>    that we may heal the shattered world,
>    and find a new and better life,
>    through Christ our Lord. Amen.

# II. The Eucharist

### 1. CANON OF THE NEW CREATION

Father, we thank you
for the great things you ask of us.

You gave us a world to build,
and mind and strength to build it.
You kept us safe with your power
until we could find our own.
You taught us to call you father
so we would learn to call each other brother and sister.

You raised up Jesus, our brother,
to be your son, the first-born of your new creation.
In him we see what we can become.
In his life our twisted and broken lives can become one.
As Jesus lived and died for us,
we can live and die for each other.

You are with us now in your spirit,
the spirit of unity, peace and love.
In this spirit we can work together
with each other and all men everywhere
to build a new world, your new creation.

> For all these things we thank you, Lord,
> as we join together in your praise:
> Holy, holy, holy, lord God of life,
> heaven and earth are filled with your glory.
> We praise you and thank you.

Holy is our brother Jesus
who revealed to us your power.
We praise you and thank you.

In this spirit of praise and thanksgiving,
in the unity, love and fellowship to which you have called us,
we are gathered here to remember
the great things you have done for us.

You freed our fathers from their superstitions,
led them out from the tyranny of Egypt,
gave them a land to build on,
and the promise of a new society.

You sent us your son,
the promise of a new life,
and victory over death.

On the night before he died
He took bread, broke it and gave it to his friends, saying:
Take this and eat.
This is my body which is to be broken for you.

Then he took a cup, gave thanks to you, and said:
Take this and drink.
This is the cup of my blood,
of the new and everlasting covenant,
which shall be shed for you and for all men
for the forgiveness of sins.
Each time you do these things,
you will be remembering me,
and sharing in the new creation.

When we eat this bread and drink from this cup
we proclaim the death of the Lord until he comes.

We remember, Lord, that Jesus lived for us,
suffered, died and rose in glory for us.
He is a sign that we can conquer death
if we will live in the power of your spirit.

In Christ's name we offer
this bread and this cup to you,
as a sign to you and to ourselves
that we are pledged to work together
with men of good will everywhere
to build a new society of peace and love
and to enter into a new life.

We pray that we may live the gospel,
loving and caring for each other,
the poor, the sick, the oppressed, and all who are in need.
We pray that we may be your people,
in peace and communion with your church
throughout the world.

The body and blood of Jesus, your son,
which we are about to share,
is the sign of our faith and our unity,
and the food of our new life together.
Through him and with him and in him
we praise you and we thank you
Lord God, our father,
together with your spirit,
today and every day until the new creation is achieved.

Amen.
Praise and glory, wisdom and thanksgiving,
honor and power and strength to our God
who makes all things new.
Amen.

## 2. AN AMERICAN CANON

Let us be at peace with one another.
>Amen.

Lift up your hearts.
>We have lifted them up to the Lord.

Let us give thanks to the Lord our God.
>It is right and just.

It is not only right, but helpful
for us to give you thanks, Father,
at all times and in all places.
We do so now through Jesus our brother,
who lived among us full of grace and truth.
He died to destroy death,
and rose that we might live forever with him.
With the church through all the ages,
and with all the angels and saints
we sing your praise and say:

>Holy, holy, holy, Lord God of hosts.

>Heaven and earth are full of your glory.

>Hosanna in the highest!

We your people,
thankful for the glorious freedom your children enjoy,
offer you this sacrifice of praise, Father,
for all the wonders you have made.
All things are good, and through your life-giving spirit
they are a source of blessing.
Send that same spirit upon the gifts we bring,
that they may become the body and blood of Christ your Son.

The night before he gave himself up for the world,
he took bread and blessed you, saying:
You are blessed, Lord God, ageless King,
for bringing bread from the earth.
He broke the bread, gave it to his friends, and told them:

Take this bread and eat it—it is my body
which is being broken for you.
        Amen.
After supper, he took a cup of wine and blessed you, saying:
You are blessed, Lord God, ageless King,
for creating the fruit of the vine.
He passed the cup among his friends and told them:
Take this and drink from it, all of you—
it is my blood that is being poured out for you and all men,
to seal a new and everlasting covenant.
Do this to remember me!
        Amen.


        We remember his death for the life of the world,
        how he rose from the dead
        and returned to the glory that was his.
        We proclaim that he will come again in splendor,
        when we shall feast with him in your kingdom.
        Blessed is he who comes in the name of the Lord.
        Hosanna in the highest!
We ask you to send your spirit among us,
that the bread we break and the cup we share
may make us one with Christ and with each other.
Grant to all men the bread of earthly reality to nourish them,
the wine of created beauty to delight them,
and the discipline of human struggle to make them strong.
        We thank you for forming man in your image
        and sustaining him in your love.
        May the families of men and nations be open to the future.
        May they learn that on earth
        your work is truly their own.
        We thank you for your church, a pilgrim like our fathers.
        May the church be the first to become conscious
        of all that the world loves, pursues and suffers,
        the first to unfold and sacrifice herself

to become more widely human and more nobly of the earth
than any of the world's servants.
We thank you for the land that is ours, your gift to us.
May she be open to the voices and dreams of all her
citizens.
Relying firmly on your providence,
may she secure your blessings of true liberty
for all men in their posterity.
We thank you for men of vision and sacrifice . . .
May we also be open to the needs of others,
and through our efforts
may they feel your presence and power.
Rest your weary ones, shelter your homeless ones,
free your imprisoned ones, comfort your lonely ones,
and show yourself to all men
as the God who gave us life and liberty.
So do we praise you and give you glory.
Answer our prayers and welcome our thankful love.
Through Christ our Lord.
To him,
whose power working within us
can do immeasurably more
than we can ask or even imagine,
to him be the glory,
in the church and in Jesus Christ,
through all generations
forever and ever. Amen.

Holy, holy, holy is the Lord God almighty.
He was, and is, and is to come.
You are our lord and our God;
you are worthy of glory, honor and power,
because you made all things,
and only because you will it
were all things made and continue to be.
Amen!

3.   CANON OF A CHRISTIAN PEOPLE

We give you praise and thanks, Almighty Father,
that you are God
creator and father of all men.
You know us and so we live.
You love us and so we are your people.

Blessed are you, Father,
that you have given us this day and this hour.
Blessed are you, Father,
in all the things you have made:
in plants and in animals
and in men, the wonders of your hand.
Blessed are you, Father,
for the food we eat;
for bread and for wine
and for laughter in your presence.
Blessed are you, Father,
that you have given us eyes to see your goodness
in the things you have made,
ears to hear your word,
hands that we may touch and bless and understand.

We give you thanks that, having made all things,
you keep them and love them.
And so, with all your creation,
we praise you through our Lord Jesus Christ, saying:
Holy, holy, holy, Lord God of Hosts
Heaven and earth are filled with your glory.
Hosannah in the highest.
Blessed is he who comes in the name of the Lord.
Hosannah in the highest.

And so we offer you, most merciful Father,
through your son Jesus Christ,
this sacrifice of praise.
You have chosen us to be your children,
You have called us to a life of joy and love:
You have given us your beloved Son.

We wish to offer you ourselves
in this, your son's most holy sacrifice.
We pray for the welfare of your church,
for our bishop . . .
for our pope . . .
for all believers
and for all unbelievers everywhere.

We remember with love the blessed virgin Mary,
mother of our Lord Jesus Christ;
we remember his holy apostles, his martyrs, and his saints.

We ask for peace everywhere on earth,
peace among all men who still do not know
that we are brothers.
We ask that, loving one another in the bonds of peace,
we may love you as your son has loved you.

Through him we praise you, Father,
through your son Jesus Christ.
He has revealed your love to us.
He is the image and the incarnation of your presence.
He has become man for us.

You sent him from heaven to a virgin's womb.
He took flesh
and was born of the virgin and of the Holy Spirit.

He did all things that were pleasing to you:
he grew and he obeyed and he loved you
even to his death for us on the cross.

Before he was handed over
to undergo the suffering he accepted for us,
thereby to free us from death and selfishness and sin,
to bring light to a darkened world,
to make a new covenant of love and mercy,
he took bread into his hands, gave thanks,
and gave it to his friends, saying:
Take this and eat.
This is my body which is to be broken for you.

In the same way, he took the cup, gave thanks,
and gave it to his friends, saying:
Take this and drink.
This is the cup of my blood,
of the new and everlasting covenant,
which shall be shed for you and for all others
for the forgiveness of sins and the promise of life forever.
Whenever you do these things,
you will be commemorating me.

And so, Lord God, we commemorate now
that he suffered and died for us
and that he is the first-born of all creation,
that he has triumphed over death and lives forever
glorious in his resurrection,
that he sits at your right hand and speaks on our behalf,
and that he will come to do justice to the living and the dead
on the day you shall appoint.

We pray that this perfect sacrifice of your son
which we offer you in humility and love
may be the sign of our surrender to you.

We pray that before the eyes of all men
we may live your Gospel
and be the sacrament of Christ's presence,
that we may support one another in love,
that our hearts may be open
to the poor, the sick, the unwanted,
to all who are in need.
We pray that thus we may truly be
the church of Jesus Christ,
serving one another out of love for you.

And so, Lord God, we eat of this body
and drink of this blood
of your son Jesus Christ
as the sign of our faith
and as the food of our life in Christ.

Through him and with him and in him
we bless you and praise you and thank you,
almighty God our Father,
together with the Holy Spirit,
now and forever. Amen.

©, John L'Heureux, 1967

4.  CANON OF THE PILGRIM CHURCH

To you, almighty father, we give thanks and praise.
For it was you that made the heavens,
the sun and the moon and the stars.
It was you that established the earth,
you that gave breath to its people.

To this people you said,
I did not make the earth to lie idle,
I made it to be your home.
And so they drew from it bread and wine,
and opened rivers in the rock.
They raised up cities from the ground,
and sang new songs in the air.

So now, with all your creation,
we give you thanks and praise,
through your son, Jesus Christ, our Lord,
he who is before all things,
and he holds all things in unity.
He was there when the morning stars sang together,
and all the angels shouted for joy.
Now we join our voices to theirs, saying:

> Holy, holy, holy, Lord God of hosts.
> Heaven and earth are filled with your glory.
> Hosanna in the highest.
> Blessed is he who comes in the name of the Lord.
> Hosanna in the highest.

> We thank you, almighty Father,
> for sending him to dwell among us,
> born of the people of Abraham
> whom you multiplied as the stars of heaven,

and the sand of the seashore;
born of the people of Moses
whom you led through the desert,
going before them in a pillar of fire and cloud;
born of the daughter of Sion,
in whom the promise of his coming was fulfilled
and the sign of our fulfillment given.


We thank you for the good news that he proclaimed,
and for all that he did in our midst.
He fed the hungry,
and said that his food was to do your will.
He gave drink to the thirsty,
and taught us to thirst for the living water.
He healed the sick,
and declared his power to forgive sins.
He let his glance fall on the lonely,
and showed us that God is love.

Above all, we thank you
for the love he bore us till the end.
Knowing that you had put everything into his hands,
that he had come from you
and that he was going back to you,
he took his place at the table,
his apostles with him, and said,
I have longed to eat this passover with you
before I suffer;
I tell you, I shall not eat it again
until it is fulfilled in the kingdom of God.


And then he took bread,
and gave thanks to you, his almighty father.
He broke the bread,
and gave it to those whom he loved, saying:

Take this, all of you, and eat.
This is my body, which is to be given for you.

In the same way, he took the cup,
and when he had given thanks,
he shared it with all who were gathered there, saying:
Take this and drink.
This is the cup of my blood,
the blood of the new and everlasting covenant,
which shall be poured out for you and for all,
for the forgiveness of sins.
Whenever you do these things,
you shall do them in memory of me.

Still in pilgrimage upon this earth,
we trace in trial and under oppression
the paths he trod,
remembering how he suffered and died for us,
and rose on the third day, just as he had said,
the firstborn from the dead,
we do not lose heart for we trust that he
will come again in all his glory
to restore and establish those who believe in him.

And so we offer you, most merciful Father,
through your beloved son,
this sacrifice of praise and thanksgiving
in union with _____ our pope, with _____, our bishop
in union with all your people.

May it be a sign of our communion
in the one perfect sacrifice of your Son.
For we know that we come from you,
and that with him we shall go back to you.

Send down upon us all, therefore your Holy Spirit
that he may make of us yet more perfectly a royal
priesthood
empowered to proclaim before all men your saving name
and to speak their names in your presence;
that he may make of us yet more truly a people striving
toward that day
when you shall be all in all, everything to everyone,
the day of our lord and savior Jesus Christ your son.

Through him, and with him, and in him,
you are blessed and praised, almighty God our father,
in the unity of the Holy Spirit,
now and forever. Amen.

## 5. CANON OF GOD'S WORK

We give you thanks, holy Father,
and we proclaim your love in our midst.
You have called us into life in your image.
When in Adam we tasted the bitter fruits of sin and death,
you remained ever faithful and
did not leave us in our despair.

> We give you thanks, God of Israel,
> who promised to Abraham, our father in the faith,
> a chosen people to be a light among the nations.
> When we were in slavery
> you raised up Moses to break our chains.
> You united us in the first paschal meal.
> You led us through the sea toward the land of freedom.
> You joined us to yourself in the alliance of mercy.
> You raised your tent among us in the desert,
> and dwelt in our sanctuary in Jerusalem.
> When we abandoned you adulterously,
> you sent your prophets to summon us
> to your love once more.

We give you thanks, eternal Father;
in the fullness of time
you sent your son to become our brother.
Born of Mary, he lived our life,
growing in wisdom, stature, and grace.
He was announced by John the Baptist;
he walked among us
and announced your presence in his word and work.
But his own received him not.
When his hour had come,
in loving obedience to you and fidelity to us,
he submitted to the power of death,

the just for the unjust.
And because he laid down his life for his brothers,
you raised him up in glory
and made him lord and savior, the new man of all men.

> We give you thanks, Father of love,
> who gave us the pentecostal spirit of your son.
> You gathered us here
> to be the beginning of a new creation.
> Through you we pass from slavery to freedom,
> from egotism to brotherhood.

In this spirit we recall the supper of the Lord.
The day before he suffered
he took bread and
lifting his eyes heavenward to you, God,
his all-powerful father,
gave you thanks by pronouncing the blessing.
He broke the bread
and gave it to his disciples, saying:
All of you, take and eat this, for this is my body.

Likewise, after the supper
he also took this glorious cup
And gave thanks to you by pronouncing the blessing
and gave it to his disciples, saying:
All of you, take and drink from this,
for this is the cup of my blood,
the blood of the new and eternal covenant,
to be poured out for you and all men,
to obtain the forgiveness of sins.
Whenever you perform these actions,
do them as a memorial of me.

We recall in gratitude this great mystery of our salvation;
the death, resurrection, and ascension of your son,
Jesus Christ, our Lord.
We offer you this sacrifice, pure, holy, and immaculate,
the sacred bread of eternal life,
and the chalice of salvation.

> Father, together with Christ our brother,
> we offer you the bread and wine of our lives,
> in home, in work, in community.
> We pray you, holy Father,
> that your spirit may protect us from sin
> and maintain us in unity.
> May this holy meal
> lead to our family banquet in the new creation,
> through Christ our Lord.
> Through him, and with him, and in him. Amen.

6.   CANON OF THE WORD OF GOD

We praise you and we bless you, eternal Father,
that in the fullness of time
you have spoken to us your saving words
of graciousness and of love.
For by the message of your son
you have called us to be your children and your friends.
And by the light of your word we are warmed
and strengthened in our darkness and loneliness.

> We bless the power of your creative word,
> which first drew out from the waters of chaos
> the rich, firm land where we now live and work,
> the word that sustains the heavens and the stars,
> and the measureless immensity of space.

> We bless the kindness of your words
> of forgiveness and of promise
> that you spoke to our first parents in their shame.

> We bless your word of hope
> that long ago summoned Abraham
> from the darkness and ignorance of unbelief
> and called him to be our true father in the faith.

> We bless your summoning word
> that raised up Moses and the prophets to bear witness
> against the infidelity and injustice of mankind
> and to cleave our hearts with the two-edged sword
> of righteousness and of truth.

But most of all we bless you for your son.
For he is your first and final word of love,
and all-encompassing wisdom, who proceeds from your lips,

the alpha and the omega, the beginning and the end.
By him we are created anew.
In him we find redemption and forgiveness of sins.
Through him we are summoned to confess the power of your
    love
and are sent forth to proclaim the good news
of our salvation in humility and in truth.
With him we die and are born to a new life.

We recall the immensity of his love for us,
which led him to stretch out his arms to embrace the cross,
that your fidelity to him and to a sinful world
might be revealed.
For the night before he suffered,
with great longing he gathered together his friends
for a final meal;
and knowing full well all that was still to come,
he looked upon them with love.
Then he took the bread that lay before them;
he praised you, his eternal Father, for your faithfulness;
and he broke the bread
and gave it to his friends with the words:
Take this. Eat it. For this is my body.
It is being given for you.
And in the same way he took the cup
and gave it to them with the words:
Take this. Share it among you.
For this is the cup of my blood,
the blood of a new and everlasting covenant,
which will be shed for you and for all men
for the forgiveness of sins.
As for you, when you do these things,
do them in memory of me.

    We recall these words in gratitude and love;
    and in obedience we ponder this mystery

of the lifting up of your son, our lord Jesus Christ,
in hope and expectation of the great day
when he shall appear again before the eyes of all men
in majesty and in might.
And in the everlasting power of his command,
we place before you here
this sign of our belief and of our trust.

We ask you to renew in us now
the spirit of your son,
that we may learn from him and from his memory
the true meaning of love
and that we may find in him
an unquenchable thirst for justice and for peace.

We pray for one another
and we ask you to bless us.
Be favorable to our pope . . .
and to our bishop . . .
and to all the pastors of your church throughout the world.
Preserve in them a concern for the unity of your flock,
that they may guide it in meekness and in truth.
Grant to us, your people,
the courage to live our lives
in the image of your son.

Increase in us a concern for those whom you love,
for the lonely, for the poor,
for the homeless, for the defenseless,
that we may labor in your name
to restore to them their rightful dignity
as your adopted sons and daughters.
Please bless our president and our land,
and keep us blameless in your sight.

So, our Father,
may you always be pleased with us,
even as you were ever pleased
to look upon the face of your son and servant,
our lord, Jesus Christ.
For through him, and with him, and in him,
you are blessed and praised, God our Father,
in the unity of the Holy Spirit,
today and all days until eternity. Amen.

## 7. CANON OF GOD'S BLESSINGS

We have to thank you almighty lord God,
that you are a God of people,
that you have not been ashamed to be called our God,
that you know us by our name,
that you keep the world in your hands.

> For you have made us
> and called us into this life
> to be united with you,
> to be your people on this earth.

> Blessed are you, maker of all that exists!
> Blessed are you, who has given us space and time to live!
> Blessed are you for the light of our eyes,
> and for the air we breathe!

We thank you for the whole of creation,
for all the works of your hands,
for all you have done in our midst,
through Jesus Christ, our lord.
Therefore we praise your majesty, almighty God,
with all the living;
therefore we bow before you
and adore you with the words:

> Holy, holy, holy lord God of all living things;
> earth and heaven are filled with your glory,
> we bless your name.
> Blessed is he who will come in the midst of his people,
> we bless your name.

Blessed are you almighty God,
Father of our Lord Jesus Christ,
blessed are you.
For before the foundations of the world
you chose us
and destined us to become your children.
You liberated us from the power of darkness
and brought us into the kingdom of your beloved son.
He is the image and shape of your glory,
for him the universe was made.
In him we have received redemption
and forgiveness of sins.

On the night on which he was handed over,
he took the bread into his hands.
He lifted his eyes to you, God, his almighty Father.
He thanked you, and broke the bread,
and he gave it to his friends with the words:
Take and eat, this is my body for you.
Thus he also took the cup,
said a prayer of thanks over it, and said:
This is the new covenant in my blood
which will be shed for you and for all
with forgiveness of sins.
Each time you drink this cup,
you will do this in memory of me.

When we eat this bread
and drink from this cup
we proclaim the death of the Lord until he comes.
Therefore, Lord, our God,
we place here this sign of our faith.
And therefore we commemorate now
that he suffered and died
but most of all that he is the first-born from the dead,

the first-born of the whole creation;
that glorified at your right hand
he speaks on our behalf;
and that he will come
to do justice to the living and the dead
on the day which you have appointed.

We pray, Lord our God,
send over us your holy spirit,
the spirit who brings to life the power of Jesus Christ.
We pray that this bread and this cup
which we offer you in humility
may really be the sign of our surrender to you.
We pray that in the midst of this world,
and before the eyes of all people with whom we are united
we may live your gospel
and be the sign of your peace;
that we may support and serve each other in love
that our hearts may be opened
to the poor, the sick and the dying,
to all who are in need.

We pray that thus we may be the church of Jesus Christ,
united with our bishop and with our pope ————,
and with all the believers everywhere on this earth.

Through him and with him and in him
you are blessed and praised,
Lord our God, almighty Father,
in the union of the Holy Spirit,
today and all days until eternity. Amen.

## 8. CANON OF CHRISTIAN UNITY

It is our joy and our salvation
to sing to you, to bless you, and to praise you,
to give you thanks and to worship you,
for you alone are our God,
You, and your only begotten son, with the Holy Spirit.
We beg you Lord never to desert your flock
but to guard and protect it always
through your blessed apostles
and those you have chosen to follow them.
You are the eternal shepherd who watches over your sheep.
Guide and direct with your spirit
those you have chosen to carry on your work.
For all your gifts we give you thanks
and with all creation proclaim the hymn of your glory:

> Holy, holy, holy, Lord God of hosts.
> Heaven and earth are filled with your glory;
> Hosanna in the highest.
> Blessed is he who comes in the name of the lord.
> Hosanna in the highest.

We give you thanks, almighty Father, and we sing your praise
for the wonderful works you have done in our midst.
You led our fathers, the children of Israel,
from the land of Egypt and set them free
from the bonds of slavery which held them captive.
You gave us, in the slaughter of the lamb, that first passover
to be a sign of our own deliverance from sin.
Through Moses you made a covenant with your people
by which you bound yourself to us in love forever.
You showed us your reward for loving trust in you
by your generous fulfillment
of the promises you made to Abraham.

Little by little, and in many different ways,
You made yourself known to us by the prophets;
Finally, in the fullness of time,
You spoke to us in a son.

This son came to us in mystery,
as a sign of contradiction to this world.
By his life, he showed us how to live.
By his love, he showed us how to love.

He did not want to leave us,
but wished to stay with us
even after his mission on earth was accomplished.
On the day before he suffered and died for us
he left us a sign
in which he would always be among us and for us.

While he was together with his friends at dinner
he took bread into his hands.
He raised his eyes to you, Father, and gave you thanks.
He blessed the bread, and gave it to his friends, saying:
Take and eat of this all of you:
This is my body which is given for you.

In the same way, as the dinner came to an end,
he took a cup of wine.
Once more he gave thanks to you, Father;
He blessed the cup, and passed it to his friends, saying:
Take this cup and drink from it:
This is the cup of my blood
The sign of my new and everlasting covenant with you.
This blood shall be shed for you and for all men
so that sins may be forgiven.
Whenever you do this, you will do it in memory of us.

Heavenly father, we give you thanks,
for the gift you have given us
in Christ Jesus, your son.
We recall his life, death and victorious resurrection.
We proclaim our faith in his presence among us.

Send your spirit upon us and these our gifts:
Grant that through them we may do honor to you
and be worthy to be called your sons.

Holy father, keep us all by your power.
Make us one, Father, as you are one
with your son and the Holy Spirit.
We do not ask you to take us from the world
but to keep us from harm.
You sent your son into this world;
So, too, he has sent us, that the world might believe.
It is not for us alone that we make this request,
but for all who come to believe in you through our word.
Let us all be one in you
that the world may believe that you sent us.

We pray again the prayer of your son, Jesus Christ,
and ask its fulfillment in his name.
It is ever through him that all good gifts
are created by you, given life, and bestowed upon us.

Through him, with him, and in him
we give you honor and glory
together with the Holy Spirit
forever and ever. Amen.

## 9. THE JESUS CANON

Dearly beloved, our faith tells us that Jesus is here with us,
as we have heard his word,
as we have been together in his name.
Now let us prepare to meet him in his banquet of love.

*A relatively long pause of silence.*

Jesus, our brother and our Lord,
in all simplicity, we want to thank you
for all that you have done for us.
We thank you for giving us this world
which you loved so much that you even became a part of it.
We thank you for coming from a prepared people
which you have broadened to include our whole human family.
We thank you for living our life, dying our death,
so we could live with your life.
We thank you for sending your spirit,
to be with the company of your disciples
in their pilgrimage across the centuries,
around this globe and even into space.
We thank you for the crowd of witnesses
that you have called up for each generation
to speak your message, love and peace.

*If anyone has any other motives or gratitudes, please feel
free to express them.*

The night before you willingly accepted death,
you ate with your friends
and taking bread you thanked our Father,
broke the bread, gave it to your disciples while saying,

"Take this and eat it. This is my body."
At the fourth cup you took the wine, thanked our Father again
and gave the cup to your friends saying,
"Take this and drink from it, all of you.
This is the cup of my blood
of the new and everlasting covenant.
This blood is to be poured out for you and all men
so that sins may be forgiven.
Do this in memory of me."

> We have done this and we believe by this simple action
> that you, the Lord of the street,
> have banished time and space
> and brought your suffering, your rising,
> and your ascension into our presence.
> Your total giving of yourself to our Father
> and his gracious acceptance of you
> have now become our means of self-giving
> and his acceptance of us.

In this spirit of generosity and shared giving
we ask you to look upon us with love and mercy.
Make us ever more loving,
ever more concerned about your whole family,
ever more faithful to your call
to be servants and peacemakers.
We are only a small portion of your church.
Look upon the total church;
make it lively where it is boring,
make it compassionate where it is unconcerned,
make it faithful where it has wandered.
And in the joy of your presence
we salute our brothers and sisters who are with you in glory,

we make a plea for peace for those who have died,
and we beg you to give solace to our war-weary world.

Lord Jesus, because we are with you and in you,
we are able to give to God, our Father,
in union with the Holy Spirit,
all honor and glory,
forever and ever. Amen.

## *III. The Meal*

LORD'S PRAYER

Our Father . . .
> for the kingdom, the power and the glory
> are yours through endless ages. Amen.

COMMUNION SONG

CONCLUDING PRAYER

BLESSING

Return now to the work that is yours.
Remember the peace and love we have celebrated
and do not fail to show to all men
the new life that is already among us.
Have courage; hold on to what is good.
Return no man evil for evil;
Strengthen those who fail; support the weak;
care for the poor and the suffering, and honor all men.
Love and serve the Lord and each other,
and be happy in the power of the spirit.

May almighty God bless you,
the father, the son and the spirit.
> Amen.

# THE READINGS

# 1

That night at the hotel, in our room with the long empty hall outside and our shoes outside the door, a thick carpet on the floor of the room, outside the windows the rain falling and in the room light and pleasant and cheerful, then the light out and it exciting with smooth sheets and the bed comfortable, feeling that we had come home, feeling no longer alone, waking in the night to find the other one there, and not gone away; all other things were unreal. We slept when we were tired and if we woke the other one woke too so one was not alone. Often a man wishes to be alone and a girl wishes to be alone too and if they love each other they are jealous of that in each other, but I can truly say we never felt that. We could feel alone when we were together, alone against the others. It has only happened to me like that once. I have been alone while I was with many girls and that is the way that you can be most lonely. But we were never lonely and never afraid when we were together. I know that the night is not the same as the day: that all things are different, that the things of the night cannot be explained in the day, because they do not then exist, and the night can be a dreadful time for lonely people once their loneliness has started. But with Catherine there was almost no difference in the night except that it was an even better time. If people bring so much courage to this world the world has to kill them to break them, so of course it kills them. The world breaks every one and afterward many are strong at the broken places. But those that will not break it kills. It kills the very good and the very gentle and the very brave impartially. If you are none of these you can be sure it will kill you too but there will be no special hurry.

ERNEST HEMINGWAY, *A Farewell to Arms*

# 2

I don't know Who—or what—put the question, I don't know when it was put. I don't even remember answering. But at some moment I did answer *Yes* to Someone—or Something—and from that hour I was certain that existence is meaningful and that, therefore, my life, in self-surrender, had a goal.

From that moment I have known what it means "not to look back," and "to take no thought for the morrow."

Led by the Ariadne's thread of my answer through the labyrinth of Life, I came to a time and place where I realized that the Way leads to a triumph which is a catastrophe, and to a catastrophe which is a triumph, that the price for committing one's life would be reproach, and that the only elevation possible to man lies in the depths of humiliation. After that, the word "courage" lost its meaning, since nothing could be taken from me.

As I continued along the Way, I learned, step by step, word by word, that behind every saying in the Gospels stands *one* man and *one* man's experience. Also behind the prayer that the cup might pass from him and his promise to drink it. Also behind each of the words from the Cross.

DAG HAMMARSKJOLD, *Markings*

# 3

. . . the "We are" paradoxically defines a new form of individualism. "We are" in terms of history, and history must reckon with this "We are," which must in its turn keep its place in history. I have need of others who have need of me and of each other. Every collective action, every form of society, supposes a discipline, and the individual, without this discipline, is only a stranger, bowed down under the weight of an inimical collectivity. But society and discipline lose their direction if they deny the "We are." I alone, in one sense, support the common dignity that I cannot allow either myself or others to debase. This individualism is in no sense pleasure; it is perpetual struggle, and, sometimes, unparalleled joy when it reaches the heights of proud compassion.

ALBERT CAMUS, *The Rebel*

# 4

The tragic beauty of the face of Christ
shines in the face of man;

the abandoned old live on
in shabby rooms, far from inner comfort.
Outside, in the street
din and purpose, the world like a fiery animal
reined in by youth. Within
a pallid tiring heart
shuffles about its dwelling.

Nothing, or so little, come of life's promise.
Out of broken men, despised minds
what does one make—
a roadside show, a graveyard of the heart?

The Christian God reproves
faithless ranting minds
crushing like upper and lower stones
all life between;
Christ, fowler of street and hedgerow
of cripples and the distempered old
—eyes blind as woodknots,
tongues tight as immigrants'—
takes in His gospel net
all the hue and cry of existence.

Heaven, of such imperfection,
wary, ravaged, wild?

Yes. Compel them in.

DANIEL BERRIGAN, *The Face of Christ*

# 5

What heartbeats, lisping like a lizard in a broken cistern,
Tell you, my prudent citizen, that you are nearly dead?
We heard your pains revolving on the axis of a shout:
The cops and doctors view the winter of your knifelong blood.

They chart the reeling of your clockwise reason
Flying in spirals to escape philosophy,
While life's ecliptic, drives you like an arrow
To the pit of pain.
And one by one your wars break up the arctic
Of your faultless logic,
And wills retreat upon themselves until the final seizure:
Your frozen understanding separates
And dies in floes.

Oh how you plot the crowflight of that cunning thief, your
    appetite,
But never see what fortunes
Turn to poison in your blood
How have you hammered all your senses into curses,
Forever twisting in your memory
The nails of sensuality and death.
Have we not seen you stand, full-armed,
And miss the heavens with the aimless rifles of your fear?

When are you going to unclench
The whited nerve of your rapacity, you cannibal:
Or draw one breath in truth and faith,
You son of Cain?

But if you are in love with fortunes, or with forgery,
Oh, learn to mint you golden courage
With the image of all Mercy's Sovereign,
Turn all your hunger to humility and to forgiveness,
Forsake your deserts of centrifugal desire:
Then ride in peaceful circles to the depths of life,
And hide you from your burning noon-day devil
Where clean rock-water dropwise spends, and dies in rings.

THOMAS MERTON, *Ode to the Present Century*

# 6

Since the world points up beauty as such,
There is ugliness too.
If goodness is taken as goodness,
Wickedness enters as well.

For is and is-not come together;
Hard and easy are complementary;
Long and short are relative;
High and low are comparative;
Pitch and sound make harmony;
Before and after are a sequence.

Indeed the Wise Man's office
Is to work by being still;
He teaches not by speech
But by accomplishment;
He does for everything,
Neglecting none;
Their life he gives to all,
Possessing none;
And what he brings to pass
Depends on no one else.
As he succeeds,
He takes no credit
And just because he does not take it,
credit never leaves him.

LAO TZU, *The Way of Life*

# 7

Now there is this song on the saxophone. And I am ashamed.
A glorious little suffering has just been born, an exemplary suffering. Four notes on the saxophone. They come and go, they
seem to say: You must be like us, suffer in rhythm. All right!
Naturally, I'd like to suffer that way, in rhythm, without com-
placence, without self-pity, with an arid purity. But is it my
fault if the beer at the bottom of my glass is warm, if there are
brown stains on the mirror, if I am not wanted, if the sincerest
of my sufferings drags and weighs, with too much flesh and the
skin too wide at the same time, like a sea-elephant, with bulging
eyes, damp and touching and yet so ugly? No, they certainly
can't tell me it's compassionate—this little jewelled pain which
spins around above the record and dazzles me. Not even ironic:
it spins gaily, completely self-absorbed; like a scythe it has cut
through the drab intimacy of the world and now it spins and all
of us, Madeleine, the thick-set man, the patronne, myself, the
tables, benches, the stained mirror, the glasses, all of us abandon
ourselves to existence, because we were among ourselves, only
among ourselves, it has taken us unawares, in the disorder, the
day to day drift: I am ashamed for myself and for what exists
*in front* of it.

JEAN PAUL SARTRE, *Nausea*

# 8

Something in us prevents us from remembering, when remembering proves to be too difficult or painful. We forget benefits, because the burden of gratitude is too heavy for us. We forget former loves, because the burden of obligations implied by them surpasses our strength. We forget former hates, because the task of nourishing them would disrupt our mind. We forget former pain, because it is still too painful. We forget guilt, because we cannot endure its sting. Such forgetting is not the natural, daily form of forgetting. It demands our cooperation. We repress what we cannot stand. We forget it by entombing it within us. Ordinary forgetting liberates us from innumerable small things in a natural process. Forgetting by repression does not liberate us, but seems to cut us off from what makes us suffer. We are not entirely successful, however, because the memory is buried within us, and influences every moment of our growth. And sometimes it breaks through its prison and strikes at us directly and painfully.

PAUL TILLICH, *The Eternal Now*

# 9

Jesus Christ belonged to the true race of prophets. He saw with open eye the mystery of the soul. Drawn by its severe harmony, ravished with its beauty, he lived in it, and had his being there. Alone in all history he estimated the greatness of man. One man was true to what is in you and me. He saw that God incarnates himself in man, and evermore goes forth anew to take possession of his World. He said, in this jubilee of sublime emotion "I am divine. Through me, God acts; through me speaks. Would you see God, see me; or see thee, when thou also thinkest as I now think." . . .

. . . And now, my brothers, you will ask, What in these desponding days can be done by us? The remedy is already declared in the ground of our complaint of the Church. . . .

. . . Let me admonish you, first of all, to go alone; to refuse the good models, even those which are sacred in the imagination of men, and dare to love God without mediator or veil. . . . Say, "I also am a man." Imitation cannot go above its model. The imitator dooms himself to hopeless mediocrity. The inventor did it because it was natural to him, and so in him it has a charm. In the imitator something else is natural, and he bereaves himself of his own beauty, to come short of another man's.

Yourself a newborn bard of the Holy Ghost, cast behind you all conformity, and acquaint men at first hand with Deity. Look to it first and only, that fashion, custom, authority, pleasure, and money, are nothing to you—are not bandages over your eyes, that you cannot see—but live with the privilege of the immeasurable mind. . . . When you meet one of these men and women, be to them a divine man; be to them thought and virtue; let their timid aspirations find in you a friend; let their trampled instincts be genially tempted out in your atmosphere; let their doubts know that you have doubted, and their wonder feel that you have wondered. By trusting your own heart, you shall gain more confidence in other men. For all our penny-wisdom, for all our soul-destroying slavery to habit, it is not to be doubted that all men have sublime thoughts; that all men value the few real hours of life; they love to be heard; they love to be caught up into the vision of principles. We mark with light in the memory the few interviews we have had, in the dreary years of routine and of sin, with souls that made our souls wiser; that spoke what we thought; that told us what we knew; that gave us leave to be what we only were. Discharge to men the priestly office, and, present or absent, you shall be followed with their love as by an angel.

RALPH WALDO EMERSON, *Harvard Divinity School Address*

# 10

What, then, is our neighbor? Thou hast regarded his thought, his feeling, as somehow different from thine. Thou has said, "A pain in him is not like a pain in me, but something far easier to bear." He seems to thee a little less living than thou; his life is dim, it is cold, it is a pale fire beside thy own burning desires. . . . So dimly and by instinct hast thou made [of him] a thing, no Self at all. Have done with this illusion, and simply try to learn the truth. Pain is pain, joy is joy, everywhere, even as in thee. In all the songs of the forest birds; in all the cries of the wounded and dying, struggling in the captor's power; in the boundless sea where the myriads of water-creatures strive and die; amid all the countless hordes of savage men; in all sickness and sorrow; in all exultation and hope, everywhere, from the lowest to the noblest, the same conscious, burning, wilful life is found, endlessly manifold as the forms of the living creatures, unquenchable as the fires of the sun, real as these impulses that even now throb in thine own selfish heart. Lift up thy eyes, behold that life, and then turn away, and forget it as thou canst; but, if thou has *known* that, thou hast begun to know thy duty."

JOSIAH ROYCE, *The Religious Aspect of Philosophy*

# 11

Man is more than a face his father yearned
over still waters. Behind that irony
carved and enclosed, soul
is personal diamond: into dark says:
stars are more than dark confuses them.

Man is more than day denies him:
all things of stone or music, setting against time
a living shoulder, a flower's stubborn
delicacy.
      Soul is a soul changed
in mid-journey to nightingale:
it sits the golden bough, unreels its voice
far even as us: I am wronged
but not silenced: I pour my light, my coals
upon just and guilty. Bear it
who can.

The dancer improvises and is hardly there:
a whirling diamond: each attitude
a universe. Our hearts cry
sensing through ease that agony: be still.
One could as well halt the heart cold.
No: he must mime life to live again.

Not invisible, but strictly contained. You must
keep vigil, but be above
lowly unexpected showings. I see him
in shape of hand, cleave and bid aside
the dark. Or with password *friend* pass
in another's eyes. Suspect tenderness
of harboring him.

DANIEL BERRIGAN, *Man Is More*

# 12

A young man, adamant in his committed life. The one who was nearest to him relates how, on the last evening, he arose from supper, laid aside his garments, and washed the feet of his friends and disciples—an adamant young man, alone as he confronted his final destiny.

He had observed their mean little play for his—his!—friendship. He knew that not one of them had the slightest conception why he had to act in the way that he must. He knew how frightened and shaken they would all be. And one of them had informed on him, and would probably soon give a signal to the police.

He had assented to a possibility in his being, of which he had had his first inkling when he returned from the desert. If God required anything of him, he would not fail. Only recently, he thought, had he begun to see more clearly, and to realize that the road of possibility might lead to the Cross. He knew, though, that he had to follow it still uncertain as to whether he was indeed "the one who shall bring it to pass," but certain that the answer could only be learned by following the road to the end. The end *might* be a death without significance—as well as being the end of the road of possibility.

Well, then, the last evening. An adamant young man: "Know ye what I have done to you? . . . And now I have told you before it come to pass. . . . One of you shall betray me. . . . Wither I go, ye cannot come. . . . Will'st thou lay down thy life for my sake? Verily I say unto thee: the cock shall not crow. . . . My peace I give unto you. . . . That the world may know that

I love the Father, and as the Father gave me commandment, even so I do. . . . Arise, let us go hence."

Is the hero of this immortal, brutally simple drama in truth "the Lamb of God that taketh away the sins of the world"? Absolutely faithful to a divined possibility—in that sense the Son of God, in that sense the sacrificial Lamb, in that sense the Redeemer. A young man, adamant in his commitment, who walks the road of possibility to the end without self-pity or demand for sympathy, fulfilling the destiny he has chosen—even sacrificing affection and fellowship when the others are unready to follow him—into a new fellowship.

DAG HAMMARSKJOLD, *Markings*

# 13

My children,
The Enlightened One, because He saw Mankind drowning
    in the Great Sea of Birth, Death and Sorrow,
    and longed to save them,
For this He was moved to pity.

Because He saw the men of the world straying in false paths,
    and none to guide them,
For this He was moved to pity.

Because He saw that they lay wallowing in the mire
    of the Five Lusts, in dissolute abandonment,
For this He was moved to pity.

Because He saw them still fettered to their wealth, . . .
    not knowing how to cast them aside,
For this He was moved to pity.

Because He saw them doing evil with hand, heart, and tongue,
    and many times receiving the bitter fruits of sin,
    yet ever yielding to their desires,
For this He was moved to pity.

Because He saw that though they longed for happiness,
    they made for themselves no karma of happiness;
    and though they hated pain, yet willingly made for
        themselves
    a karma of pain; and though they coveted the joys of
        Heaven,
    would not follow His commandments on earth,
For this He was moved to pity.

Because He saw them afraid of birth, old age and death,
    yet still pursuing the works that lead
    to birth, old age and death,
For this He was moved to pity.

Because He saw them consumed by the fires
    of pain and sorrow, yet knowing not where to seek
    the still waters of samadhi,
For this He was moved to pity.

Because He saw them living in an evil time, subjected to
    tyrannous kings and suffering many ills,
    yet heedlessly following after pleasure,
For this He was moved to pity.

Because He saw them living in a time of wars, killing, and
    wounding one another; and knew that for the riotous
        hatred
    hatred that had flourished in their hearts
    they were doomed to pay an endless retribution,
For this He was moved to pity.

Because many born at the time of His incarnation had heard
    Him preach the Holy Law, yet could not receive it,
For this He was moved to pity.

Because some had great riches that they could not bear
    to give away,
For this He was moved to pity.

Because He saw the men of the world ploughing their fields,
    sowing the seed, trafficking, huckstering, buying and
    selling; and at the end winning nothing but bitterness,
For this He was moved to pity.

BUDDHA'S *Pity*

# 14

Today the challenge of political courage looms larger than ever before. For our everyday life is becoming so saturated with the tremendous power of mass communications that any unpopular or unorthodox course arouses a storm of protests such as John Quincy Adams—under attack in 1807—could never have envisioned. Our political life is becoming so expensive, so mechanized and so dominated by professional politicians and public relations men that the idealist who dreams of independent statesmanship is rudely awakened by the necessities of election and accomplishment. And our public life is becoming so increasingly centered upon that seemingly unending war to which we have given the curious epithet "cold" that we tend to encourage rigid ideological unity and orthodox patterns of thought.

And thus, in the days ahead, only the very courageous will be able to take the hard and unpopular decisions necessary for our survival . . . And only the very courageous will be able to keep alive the spirit of individualism and dissent which gave birth to this nation, nourished it as an infant and carried it through its severest tests upon the attainment of its maturity.

Of course, it would be much easier if we could all continue to think in traditional political patterns—of liberalism and conservatism, as Republicans and Democrats, from the viewpoint of North and South, management and labor, business and consumer or some equally narrow framework. It would be more comfortable to continue to move and vote in platoons, joining whomever of our colleagues are equally enslaved by some current fashion, raging prejudice or popular movement. But today this nation cannot tolerate the luxury of such lazy political habits. Only the strength and progress and peaceful change that come from independent judgment and individual ideas—and even from the unorthodox and the eccentric—can enable us to surpass that foreign ideology that fears free thought more than it fears hydrogen bombs.

JOHN F. KENNEDY, *Profiles in Courage*

# 15

The youth cringed as if discovered in a crime. By heavens, they had won after all! The imbecile line had remained and become victors. He could hear cheering.

He lifted himself upon his toes and looked in the direction of the fight. A yellow fog lay wallowing on the treetops. From beneath it came the clatter of musketry. Hoarse cries told of an advance.

He turned away amazed and angry. He felt that he had been wronged.

He had fled, he told himself, because annihilation approached. He had done a good part in saving himself, who was a little piece of the army. He had considered the time, he said, to be one in which it was the duty of every little piece to rescue itself if possible. Later the officers could fit the little pieces together again, and make a battle front. If none of the little pieces were wise enough to save themselves from the flurry of death at such a time, why, then, where would be the army? It was all plain that he had proceeded according to very correct and commendable rules. His actions had been sagacious things. They had been full of strategy. They were the work of a master's legs.

Thoughts of his comrades came to him. The brittle blue line had withstood the blows and won. He grew bitter over it. It seemed that the blind ignorance and stupidity of those little pieces had betrayed him. He had been overturned and crushed by their lack of sense in holding the position, when intelligent deliberation would have convinced them that it was impossible. He, the enlightened man who looks afar in the dark, had fled because of his superior perceptions and knowledge.

STEPHEN CRANE, *The Red Badge of Courage*

# 16

And an old priest said, Speak to us of Religion.

And he said: Have I spoken this day of aught else?

Is not religion all deeds and all reflection, and that which is neither deed nor reflection, but a wonder and a surprise ever springing in the soul, even while the hands hew the stone and tend the loom?

Who can separate his faith from his actions, or his belief from his occupation?

Who can spread his hours before him, saying: "This for God and this for myself; this for my soul, and this other for my body?"

All your hours are wings that beat through space from self to self.

He who wears his morality but as his best garment were better naked.

The wind and the sun will tear no holes in his skin.

And he who defines his conduct by ethics imprisons his songbird in a cage.

The freest song comes not through bars and wires.

And he to whom worshipping is a window, to open but also to shut, has not yet visited the house of his soul whose windows are from dawn to dawn.

Your daily life is your temple and your religion.

Whenever you enter into it take with you your all.

Take the plough and the forge and the mallet and the lute, the things you have fashioned in necessity or for delight.

For in revery you cannot rise above your achievements nor fall lower than your failures.

And take with you all men:

For in adoration you cannot fly higher than their hopes nor humble yourself lower than their despair.

And if you would know God be not therefore a solver

of riddles. Rather look about you and you shall see him
playing with your children.

And look into space; you shall see Him walking in the
cloud,
outstretching His arms in the lightning and descending in rain.

You shall see Him smiling in flowers, then rising
and waving His hands in trees.

KAHLIL GIBRAN, *The Prophet*

# 17

I was the Widow McFarlane,
Weaver of carpets for all the village.
And I pity you still at the loom of life,
You who are singing to the shuttle
And lovingly watching the work of your hands,
If you reach the day of hate, of terrible truth.
For the cloth of life is woven, you know,
To a pattern hidden under the loom—
A pattern you never see!
And you weave high-hearted, singing, singing,
You guard the threads of love and friendship
For noble figures in gold and purple.
And long after other eyes can see
You have woven a moon-white strip of cloth,
You laugh in your strength, for Hope o'erlays it
With shapes of love and beauty.
The loom stops short! The pattern's out!
You're alone in the room! You have woven a
    shroud!
And hate of it lays you in it!

EDGAR LEE MASTERS, *Widow McFarlane*

# 18

Today I saw a woman wrapped in rags
Leaping along the beach to curse the sea.
Her child lay floating in the oil, away
From oarlock, gunwale, and the blades of oars.
The skinny lifeguard, raging at the sky,
Vomited sea, and fainted on the sand.

The cold simplicity of evening falls
Dead on my mind.
And underneath the piles the water
Leaps up, leaps up, and sags down slowly, farther
Than seagulls disembodied in the drag
Of oil and foam.

Plucking among the oyster shells a man
Stares at the sea, that stretches on its side.
Now far along the beach, a hungry dog
Announces everything I knew before;
Obliterate naiads weeping underground,
Where Homer's tongue thickens with human howls.

I would do anything to drag myself
Out of this place:
Root up a seaweed from the water,
To stuff it in my mouth, or deafen me,
Free me from all the force of human speech;
Go drown, almost.

Warm in the pleasure of the dawn I came
To sing my song

And look for mollusks in the shallows,
The whorl and coil that pretty up the earth,
While far below us, flaring in the dark,
The stars go out.

What did I do to kill my time today,
After the woman ranted in the cold,
The mellow sea, the sound blown dark as wine?
After the lifeguard rose up from the waves
Like a sea-lizard with the scales washed off?
Sit there, admiring sunlight on a shell?

Abstract with terror of the shell, I stared
Over the waters where
God brooded for the living all one day.
Lonely for weeping, starved for a sound of mourning,
I bowed my head, and heard the sea far off
Washing its hands.

JAMES WRIGHT, *At the Slackening of the Tide*

# 19

Hello, darkness, my ol' friend
I've come to talk with you again
Because a vision softly creeping
Left its seeds while I was sleeping
And the vision that was planted in my brain
Still remains within the sounds of silence

In restless dreams I walked along
Narrow streets of cobblestones

With the heel of a street lamp
I turned my collar to the cold and damp
When my eyes were stabbed
By the flash of neon light
Stood the night
'n touched the sounds of silence

And in the naked light I saw
Ten thousand people—maybe more
People talking without speaking
People hearing without listening
People writing songs
That voices never share—No one dare
Disturb the sound of silence

Who said—I do not know
Silence like a cancer grows
Hears my words that I might teach you
Take my arms that I might reach you
But my words like silent raindrops fell
Echoing the sound of silence

And the people bow and prayed
To the neon god they made
And the sign flashed out its warning
In the words that it was forming
And the sign said:
"The words of the prophets are written on the subway walls
Tenement halls"
Whispered in the Sounds of Silence

SIMON AND GARFUNKLE, *Sounds of Silence*

# 20

Did anybody ever come back from the dead any single one of the millions who got killed did any one of them ever come back and say by god I'm glad I'm dead because death is always better than dishonor? Did they say I'm glad I died to make the world safe for democracy? Did they say I like death better than losing liberty? Did any of them ever say it's good to think I got my guts blown out for the honor of my country? Did any of them ever say look at me I'm dead but I died for decency and that's better than being alive? Did any of them ever say here I am I've been rotting for two years in a foreign grave but it's wonderful to die for your native land? Did any of them say hurray I died for womanhood and I'm happy see how I sing even though my mouth is choked with worms?

Nobody but the dead know whether all these things people talk about are worth dying for or not. And the dead can't talk. So the words about noble deaths and sacred blood and honor and such are all put into dead lips by grave robbers and fakes who have no right to speak for the dead. If a man says death before dishonor he is either a fool or a liar because he doesn't know what death is. He isn't able to judge. He only knows about living. He doesn't know anything about dying. If he is a fool and believes in death before dishonor let him go ahead and die. But all the little guys who are too busy to fight should be left alone. And all the guys who say death before dishonor is pure bull the important thing is life before death they should be left alone too. Because the guys who say life isn't worth living without some principle so important you're willing to die for it they are all nuts. And the guys who say you'll see there'll come a time you can't escape you're going to have to fight and die because it'll mean your very life why they are also nuts. They are talking like fools. They are saying that two and two make nothing. They are saying that a man will have to die in order to protect his life. If you agree to fight you agree to die. Now if you die to protect your life you aren't alive anyhow so how is there any sense in a thing like that? A man doesn't say I will starve myself to death to keep from starving. He doesn't say I will spend all my money in order to save my money. He doesn't say I will burn my house down in order to keep it from burning. Why then should he be willing to die for the privilege of living? There ought to be at least as much common sense about living and dying as there is about going to the grocery store and buying a loaf of bread.

DALTON TRUMBO, *Johnny Got His Gun*

# 21

I rested on that day, with a sense of widening vision, and with what it is surely fair to call an increase of religious insight into life. In God's eyes the differences of social position, of intellect, of culture, of cleanliness, of dress which different men exhibit, and all the other rarities and exceptions on which they so fantastically pin their pride, must be so small as practically to vanish; and all that should remain is the common fact that here we are, a countless multitude of vessels of life, each of us pent into peculiar difficulties, with which we must severally struggle by using whatever fortitude and goodness we can summon up. The exercise of courage, patience and kindness, must be the significant portion of the whole business; and the distinctions of position can only be a manner of diversifying the phenomenal surface upon which these underground virtues may manifest their effects. At this rate, the deepest human life is everywhere, is eternal. . . .

. . . Some of you are, perhaps, more livingly aware than you were an hour ago of the depths of worth that lie around you, hid in alien lives. And when you ask how much sympathy you ought to bestow, although the amount is, truly enough, a matter of ideal on your part, yet in this notion of the combination of ideals with active virtues you have a rough standard for shaping your decision. In any case, your imagination is extended. You divine in the world about you matter for a little more humility on your own part, and tolerance, reverence, and love for others; and you gain a certain inner joyfulness at the increased importance of our common life. Such joyfulness is a religious inspiration.

WILLIAM JAMES, *Pragmatism and Other Essays*

# 22

In our monasteries the monks busied themselves in translating, copying, and even composing such poems—under the Tartars. There is, for instance, one such poem (of course, from the Greek) *The Wanderings of Our Lady through Hell*, with descriptions as bold as Dante's. Our Lady visits Hell, and the Archangel leads her through the torments. She sees the sinners and their punishment. There she sees among others a set of sinners in a burning lake. Some of them sink to the bottom of the lake so that they can't swim out, and 'these God forgets'—an expression of extraordinary depth and force. And so Our Lady, shocked and weeping, falls before the throne of God and begs for mercy for all in Hell—for all she has seen there, and indiscriminately. Her conversation with God is most interesting. She begs Him, she will not stop. And when God points to the hands and feet of her Son, nailed to the Cross, and asks: "How can I forgive His tormentors?", she bids all the saints, all the martyrs, all the angels and archangels to fall down with her and pray for mercy for all without discrimination. It ends by her winning from God a respite from suffering every year from Good Friday till Trinity day. And the sinners at once raise a cry of thankfulness from Hell, chanting: "You are just, O Lord, in this judgment."

FYODOR DOSTOYEVSKY, *The Brothers Karamazov*

# 23

A winter's day
in a deep and dark December,
I am alone
gazing from my window to the streets below
on a freshly fallen silent shroud of snow.

> I am a rock.
> I am an island.

I build walls,
a fortress deep and mighty,
that none may penetrate.
I have no need of friendship.
Friendship causes pain
It's laughter and it's loving I disdain.

> I am a rock.
> I am an island.

Don't talk of love.
Well, I've heard the word before.
It's sleeping in my memory.
I won't disturb the slumber of feelings that have died
If I never loved, I never would have cried.

> I am a rock.
> I am an island.

I have my books and my poetry to protect me.
I am shielded in my armor.
Hiding in my room,
safe within my tomb,
I touch no one, and no one touches me.

>I am a rock.
>I am an island.

And a rock feels no pain.
And an island never cries.

SIMON AND GARFUNKEL, *I Am a Rock*

# 24

And Wisdom opened her lips and spoke:

"You, Man, would see the world with the eyes of God, and would grasp the secrets of the hereafter by means of human thought. Such is the fruit of ignorance.

"Go into the field, and see how the bee hovers over the sweet flowers and the eagle swoops down on its prey. Go into your neighbor's house and see the infant child bewitched by the firelight, while the mother is busied at her tasks. Be like the bee, and do not waste your spring days gazing on the doings of the eagle. Be like the child rejoicing at the firelight and let the mother be. All that you see was, and still is, yours.

"The many books and strange figures and the lovely thoughts around you are ghosts of the spirits that have been before you. The words your lips utter are the links in the chain that binds you and your fellow men. The sorrowful and joyful conclusions are the seeds sown by the past in the field of your soul to be reaped by the future.

"The youth that toys with your desires is he who will open the gate of your heart for Light to enter. The earth that opens wide her mouth to swallow man and his works is the redeemer of our souls from bondage to our bodies.

"The world that moves with you is your heart, which is the world itself. And Man, whom you deem so small and ignorant, is God's messenger who has come to learn the joy of life through sorrow and gain knowledge from ignorance."

Thus spoke Wisdom, and laid a hand upon my burning brow, saying:

"March on. Do not tarry. To go forward is to move toward perfection. March on, and fear not the thorns or the sharp stones on Life's path."

KAHIL GIBRAN, *The Prophet*

# 25

Where is the marvelous thief
Who stole harvest from the angry sun
And sacked with his bright sight, the land?

Where he lies dead, the quiet earth unpacks him
And wind is waving in the earth's revenge:
Fields of barley, oats and rye.

Where is the millionaire
Who squandered the bright spring?
Whose lies played in the summer evening sky
Like cheap guitars?
Who spent the golden fortunes of the fall
And died as bare as a tree?

His heart lies open like a treasury,
Filled up with grass, and generous flowers.

Where is the crazy gambler
Amid the nickels of whose blood have fallen
Heavy half-dollars of his last of life?
Where is he gone?

The burning bees come walk, as bright as jewels
Upon that flowering, dark sun:
The bullet wound in his unmoving lung.

Oh you who hate the gambler or his enemy,
Remember how the bees
Pay visits to the patient dead
And borrow honey from their charitable blood.

You who have judged the gambler or his enemy
Remember this, before the proud world's funeral.

THOMAS MERTON, *Dirge for the Proud World*

# 26

Then we understand that rebellion cannot exist without a strange form of love. Those who find no rest in God or in history are condemned to live for those who, like themselves, cannot live, in fact, for the humiliated. The most pure form of the movement of rebellion is thus crowned with the heart-rending cry of Karamazov: if all are not saved, what good is the salvation of one only? Thus Catholic prisoners, in the prison cells of Spain, refuse communion today because the priests of the regime have made it obligatory in certain prisons. These lonely witnesses to the crucifixion of innocence also refuse salvation if it must be paid for by injustice and oppression. This insane generosity is the generosity of rebellion, which unhesitatingly gives the strength of its love and without a moment's delay refuses injustice. Its merit lies in making no calculations, distributing everything it possesses to life and to living men. It is thus that it is prodigal in its gifts to men to come. Real generosity toward the future lies in giving all to the present.

Rebellion proves in this way that it is the very movement of life and that it cannot be denied without renouncing life. Its purest outburst, on each occasion, gives birth to existence. Thus it is love and fecundity or it is nothing at all. Revolution without honor, calculated revolution which, in preferring an abstract concept of man to a man of flesh and blood, denies existence as many times as is necessary, puts resentment in the place of love. Immediately rebellion, forgetful of its generous origins, allows itself to be contaminated by resentment; it denies life, dashes toward destruction, and raises up the grimacing cohorts of petty rebels, embryo slaves all of them, who end by offering themselves for sale, today, in all the marketplaces of Europe, to no matter what form of servitude. It is no longer either revolution or rebellion but rancor, malice, and tyranny. Then, when revolution in the name of power and of history becomes a murderous and immoderate mechanism, a new rebellion is consecrated in the name of moderation and of life. We are at that extremity now. At the end of this tunnel of darkness, however, there is inevitably a light, which we already divine and for which we have only to fight to ensure its coming. All of us, among the ruins, are preparing a renaissance beyond the limits of nihilism. But few of us know it.

ALBERT CAMUS, *The Rebel*

# 27

Do you remember, passer-by, the path
I wore across the lot where now stands the opera
  house,
Hasting with swift feet to work through many years?
Take its meaning to heart:
You too may walk, after the hills at Miller's Ford
Seem no longer far away;
Long after you see them near at hand,
Beyond four miles of meadow;
And after woman's love is silent,
Saying no more: "I will save you."
And after the faces of friends and kindred
Become as faded photographs, pitifully silent,
Sad for the look which means: "We cannot help you."
And after you no longer reproach mankind
With being in league against your soul's uplifted
  hands—
Themselves compelled at midnight and at noon
To watch with steadfast eye their destinies;
After you have these understandings, think of me
And of my path, who walked therein and knew
That neither man nor woman, neither toil,
Nor duty, gold nor power
Can ease the longing of the soul,
The loneliness of the soul!

EDGAR LEE MASTERS, *James Garber*

# 28

I am often on guard over the Russians. In the darkness one sees their forms move like sick storks, like great birds. They come close up to the wire fence and lean their faces against it; their fingers hook round the mesh. Often many stand side by side, and breathe the wind that comes down from the moors and the forest.

They rarely speak and then only a few words. They are more human and more brotherly towards one another, it seems to me, than we are. But perhaps that is merely because they feel themselves to be more unfortunate than us. Anyway the war is over so far as they are concerned. But to wait for dysentery is not much of a life either.

The Territorials who are in charge of them say that they were much more lively at first. They used to have intrigues among themselves, as always happens, and it would often come to blows and knives. But now they are quite apathetic, and listless.

They stand at the wire fence; sometimes one goes away and then another at once takes his place in the line. Most of them are silent; occasionally one begs a cigarette butt.

I see their dark forms, their beards move in the wind. I know nothing of them except that they are prisoners, and that is exactly what troubles me. Their life is obscure and guiltless;—if I could know more of them, what their names are, how they live, what they are waiting for, what are their burdens, then my emotion would have an object and might become sympathy. But as it is I perceive behind them only the suffering of the creature, the awful melancholy of life and the pitilessness of men.

A word of command has made these silent figures our enemies; a word of command might transform them into our friends. At some table a document is signed by some persons whom none of us knows, and then for years together that very crime on which formerly the world's condemnation and severest penalty fell, becomes our highest aim. But who can draw such a distinction when he looks at these quiet men with their child-like faces and apostles' beards. Any non-commissioned officer is more of an enemy to a recruit, any schoolmaster to a pupil than they are to us. And yet we would shoot at them again and they at us if they were free.

ERICH MARIA REMARQUE, *All Quiet on the Western Front*

# 29

Faulkner: Our final wish is to have scribbled on the wall our "Kilroy was here."

The last ditch of the enemy. We can sacrifice ourselves completely to that which is beyond and above us—and *still* hope that the memory of our choice shall remain tied to our name or, at least, that future generations shall understand why and how we acted. At times it seems to us that the bitterness we feel when we fail at an attempted task lies in this: that our failure will condemn our efforts themselves to oblivion.

O contradiction! O last stand! If only the goal can justify the sacrifice, how, then, can you attack a shadow of importance to the question whether or not the memory of your efforts will be associated with your name? If you do, is it not all too obvious that you are still being influenced in your actions by that vain dead dream about "posterity"?

DAG HAMMARSKJOLD, *Markings*

# 30

The western land, nervous under the beginning change. The Western States, nervous as horses before a thunder storm. The great owners, nervous, sensing a change, knowing nothing of the nature of the change. The great owners, striking at the immediate thing, the widening government, the growing labor unity; striking at new taxes, at plans; not knowing these things are results, not causes. Results, not causes; results, not causes. The causes lie deep and simply—the causes are a hunger in a stomach, multiplied a million times; a hunger in a single soul, hunger for joy and some security, multiplied a million times; muscles and mind aching to grow, to work, to create, multiplied a million times. The last clear definite function of man— muscles aching to work, minds aching to create beyond the single need—this is man. To build a wall, to build a house, a dam, and in the wall and house and dam to put something of Manself, and to Manself take back something of the wall, the house, the dam; to take hard muscles from the lifting, to take the clear lines and form from conceiving. For man, unlike any other thing organic or inorganic in the universe, grows beyond his work, walks up the stairs of his concepts, emerges ahead of his accomplishments. This you may say of man—when theories change and crash, when schools, philosophies, when narrow dark alleys of thought, national, religious, economic, grow and disintegrate, man reaches, stumbles forward, painfully, mistakenly sometimes. Having stepped forward, he may slip back, but only half a step, never the full step back. This you may say and know it and know it. This you may know when the bombs plummet out of the black planes on the market place, when prisoners are stuck like pigs, when the crushed bodies drain filthily in the dust. You may know it in this way.

If the step were not being taken, if the stumbling-forward ache were not alive, the bombs would not fall, the throats would not be cut. Fear the time when the bombs stop falling while the bombers live—for every bomb is proof that the spirit has not died. And fear the time when the strikes stop while the great owners live—for every little beaten strike is proof that the step is being taken. And this you can know—fear the time when Manself will not suffer and die for a concept, for this one quality is the foundation of Manself, and this one quality is man, distinctive in the universe.

JOHN STEINBECK, *The Grapes of Wrath*

# 31

How can the American Negro past be used? It is entirely possible that this dishonored past will rise up soon to smite all of us. There are some wars, for example (if anyone on the globe is still mad enough to go to war) that the American Negro will not support, however many of his people may be coerced—and there is a limit to the number of people any government can put in prison, and a rigid limit indeed to the practicality of such a course. A bill is coming in that I fear America is not prepared to pay. "The problem of the twentieth century," wrote W. E. B. Du Bois around sixty years ago, "is the problem of the color line." A fearful delicate problem, which compromises, when it does not corrupt, all the American efforts to build a better world—here, there, or anywhere. It is for this reason that everything white Americans think they believe in must now be reëxamined. What one would not like to see again is the consolidation of peoples on the basis of their color. But as long as we in the West place on color the value that we do, we make it impossible for the great unwashed to consolidate themselves according to any other principle. Color is not a human or a personal reality; it is a political reality. But this is a distinction so extremely hard to make that the West has not been able to make it yet. And at the center of this dreadful storm, this vast confusion, stand the black people of this nation, who must now share the fate of a nation that has never accepted them, to which they were brought in chains. Well, if this is so, one has no choice but to do all in one's power to change that fate, and at no matter what risk—eviction, imprisonment, torture, death. For the sake of one's children, in order to minimize the bill that *they* must pay, one must be careful not to take refuge in any delusion—and the value placed on the color of the skin is always and everywhere and forever a delusion. I know that what I am asking is impossible. But in our time, as in every time, the impossible is the least that one can demand—and one is, after all, emboldened by the spectacle of human history in general, and American Negro history in particular, for it testifies to nothing less than the perpetual achievement of the impossible.

When I was very young, and was dealing with my buddies in those wine- and urine-stained hallways, something in me wondered, *What will happen to all that beauty?* For black people, though I am aware that some of us, black and white, do not know it yet, are very beautiful. And when I sat at Elijah's table and watched the baby, the women, and the men, and we talked about God's—or Allah's—vengeance, I wondered, when that vengeance was achieved, *What will happen to all that beauty then?* I could also see that the intransigence and ignorance of the white world might make that vengeance inevitable—a vengeance that does not really depend on, and cannot really be executed by, any person or organization, and that cannot be prevented by any police force or army: historical vengeance, a cosmic vengeance, based on the law that we recognize when we say, "Whatever goes up must come down." And here we are, at the center of the arc, trapped in the gaudiest, most valuable, and most improbable water wheel the world has ever seen. Everything now, we must assume, is in our hands; we have no right to assume otherwise. If we—and now I mean the relatively conscious whites and the relatively conscious blacks, who must, like lovers, insist on, or create, the consciousness of the others—do not falter in our duty now, we may be able, handful that we are, to end the racial nightmare, and achieve our country, and change the history of the world. If we do not now dare everything, the fulfillment of that prophecy, recreated from the Bible in song by a slave, is upon us: *God gave Noah the rainbow sign, No more water, the fire next time!*

JAMES BALDWIN, *The Fire Next Time*

# 32

How selfish and aesthetic our so-called "sympathy" usually is. There come times when, momentarily, we can serve as the foundation for somebody else's faith in himself—a faith which is constantly being threatened in all of us. When this happens, what we do to make it possible for him to "go on," we make the foundation for our own life-preserving self-esteem.

In this matter—as in many others—realism is the opposite of desecration. The truth we have to endure is our present reality without the justification which time may provide.

DAG HAMMARSKJOLD, *Markings*

# THE SONGS

# 1. Allelu

RAY REPP

Chorus: Allelu! Allelu!
Everybody sing Allelu!
The Lord has risen it is true:
Everybody sing Allelu!

1) God said he would send his Son, Allelu, Allelu!
And salvation would be won, Alleluia!

2) Christ was born in Bethlehem, Allelu, Allelu!
So that man would live again, Alleluia!

3) Thirty years he walked the land, Allelu, Allelu!
To all in need he lent his hand, Alleluia!

4) On the hard wood of the cross, Allelu, Allelu!
He suffered and he died for us, Alleluia!

5) On the third day he did rise, Allelu, Allelu!
Now he lives no more to die, Alleluia!

6) Now we too can live anew, Allelu, Allelu!
Live in him need all we do, Alleluia!

## 2. Battle Hymn of the Republic

Chorus:    Glory, glory, hallelujah!
Glory, glory, hallelujah!
Glory, glory, hallelujah!
His truth is marching on.

1) Mine eyes have seen the glory of the coming of the Lord;
He is trampling out the vintage where the grapes of wrath are stored;
He hath loosed the fateful lightning of his terrible swift sword,
His truth is marching on.

2) He has sounded forth the trumpet that shall never call retreat;
He is sifting out the hearts of men before His judgment seat;
Oh be swift, my soul, to answer Him! Be jubilant my feet!
Our God is marching on.

3) In the beauty of the lilies Christ was born across the sea,
With a glory in his bosom that transfigures you and me;
As he died to make men holy, let us die to make men free,
While God is marching on.

# 3. Bless the Lord

CLARENCE RIVERS

Chorus:    Glory to God, glory,
              O praise him, alleluia!
              Glory to God, glory,
              O praise the name of the Lord.

1) Bless the Lord, all you works of the Lord.
Praise and glorify him forever.

2) Sun and moon, bless the Lord.
Bless the Lord, you stars of heaven.

3) Fire and heat, bless the Lord.
Bless the Lord, you frost and cold.

4) Dew and rain, bless the Lord.
Bless the Lord, you ice and snow.

5) Light and darkness, bless the Lord.
Bless the Lord, you nights and days.

6) Lightnings and clouds, bless the Lord.
Bless the Lord, you winds of heaven.

7) Now let the earth bless the Lord.
Praise and glorify him forever.

8) Mountains and hills, bless the Lord.
Bless the Lord, you growing trees.

9) Springs of the earth, bless the Lord.
Bless the Lord, you seas and rivers.

10) Creatures of the sea, bless the Lord.
    Bless the Lord, you birds of the air.

11) Creatures wild and tame, bless the Lord.
    Praise and glorify him forever.

12) Now let the Church bless the Lord.
    Let his people praise his name.

13) Priests of the Lord, bless the Lord.
    Praise his name both night and day.

14) Souls of the just, bless the Lord.
    Bless the Lord, you humble of heart.

15) Bless the Lord, you saints of the Lord.
    Peoples near and far, praise his name.

16) Praise to the Father and to the Son,
    To the Holy Spirit, Three in One.

# 4. Clap Your Hands

RAY REPP

Chorus:  All you peoples, clap your hands,
    And shout for joy:
    The Lord has made all mankind one,
    So raise your voices high!

1) All creation shows the glory of the Lord;
The earth proclaims his handiwork; the sky cries out his word.
Night and day sing out the glories all about,
So praise the Lord with shouts of joy.

2) The strength of God is great; he rules from sea to sea,
And all creation knows the might and glory of his deeds.
So ev'ry queen and king, join in now as we sing,
And praise the Lord with shouts of joy.

3) The King of all the earth has made his message known,
That we should offer him ourselves and ev'rything we own.
We do this by the way we live through ev'ry day,
So live each day in peace and joy.

4) The kingdom of the Lord was made for all the good,
Those who want to live in peace and brotherhood.
So with your fellow man let's all join hand to hand,
And praise the Lord with shouts of joy.

5) Let ev'ry man alive remember your command,
That ev'ry day in ev'ry way we love our fellow man.
If this command is done, the vict'ry will be won,
And we'll all live in peace and joy.

# 5. Come Away

RAY REPP

Chorus:  Come away to the land of freedom,
          Come away, come away.
          To a land where all men are as brothers,
          Come away, come away, come away.

1)  God made a land to love in;
    Come away, come away;
    It's not too far if you do want it;
    Come away, come away, come away.

2)  The land is flowing with all riches,
    Come away, come away;
    Happiness and other such wishes;
    Come away, come away, come away.

3)  If you want to find that land now,
    Come away, come away;
    Just take my hand and you're half way there now;
    Come away, come away, come away.

4)  Side by side we'll walk together;
    Come away, come away;
    And all the way we'll love each other;
    Come away, come away, come away.

# 6. Emmanuel

NIEL BLUNT AND FRANK EIMER

Chorus:    Our Father's love has sent you here;
           O Christ, you have come to stay.
           Living through our new-born selves,
           You live and work with us today.

1)   You came for the world's new dawning,
     To a darkened selfish world;
     You brought us the light, a bright new ray
     Of your being here to stay.

2)   You came to a starving world;
     You came as the bread of life;
     You gave us your flesh, a life-filled sign
     Of your presence here to stay.

3)   You're here in our human world;
     You share your life with all;
     We find in our brotherhood the truth
     That you have come to stay.

# 7. Forevermore

RAY REPP

Chorus:  Praise to the Lord for He is good, all nations;
Join we now in the love of the Lord forevermore.

1)  In the very beginning God created man,
Gave to him all the fruits of the land,
But he gave much more
For he wanted him to live forevermore.

2)  Ungrateful man turned from God one day,
And in doing this he also gave his gifts away,
But our Father said he'd send his Son
So we could live forevermore.

3)  God the Son became a man to show us how to live,
And upon the cross the God-man's life he did give,
But in dying he did rise
That we all might live forevermore.

4)  In the bread he gave to us, all now are one,
For the bread is Christ Himself, God's only Son.
May we love each other well,
That we may live forevermore.

5)  God the Son said he must go to make a place for us,
Which would be for all good men who've lived a life
that's just,

Said he'd come again to take us there
That all might live forevermore.

# 8. Go Tell It on the Mountain

Chorus:   Go tell it on the mountain,
          Over the hills and everywhere;
          Go tell it on the mountain,
          To let my people go.

1)   Who's that yonder dressed in red?
     Let my people go.
     Must be the people that Moses led.
     Let my people go.
     Who's that yonder dressed in red?
     Must be the people that Moses led.
     Go tell it on the mountain to let my people go.

2)   Who's that yonder dressed in white?
     Let my people go.
     Must be the children of the Israelite.
     Let my people go.
     Who's that yonder dressed in White?
     Must be the children of the Israelite.
     Go tell it on the mountain to let my people go.

3)   Who's that yonder dressed in black?
     Let my people go.
     Must be the hypocrites turning back.
     Let my people go.
     Who's that yonder dressed in black?
     Must be the hypocrites turning back.
     Go tell it on the mountain to let my people go.

# 9. God Is Love

CLARENCE RIVERS

Chorus:  God is love,
And he who abides in love
Abides in God
And God in him.

1) The love of Christ has gathered us together.
Let us rejoice in him and be glad.

2) By this shall all know that we are his disciples,
If we have love one for another.

3) Owe no man anything except to love one another.
For he who loves his neighbor will fulfill the whole law.

4) O carry one another's burdens,
And so you will fulfill the law of Christ.

5) The cup of blessing which we bless,
Is it not fellowship in the blood of Christ?

6) The Bread which we break,
Is it not fellowship in the body of Christ?

7) We many are one bread, one body,
For we all partake of the one Bread.

8) This is the Bread that came down from heaven.
He who eats this Bread shall live forever!

9) We who eat his flesh and drink his blood have life
everlasting,
And he will raise us up, on the last day.

10) He is the vine, we the branches.
We who abide in him shall bear fruit.

# 10. Gonna Sing, My Lord

JOSEPH WISE

1) Gonna sing, my Lord, for all that I'm worth;
   Gonna sing, my Lord, for all that I'm worth, Lord, Lord.
   Gonna sing, my Lord, for all that I'm worth;
   Gonna sing, my Lord, Lord, Lord—till I see your face.

2) Gonna love, my Lord, for all that I'm worth;
   . . .

3) Gonna laugh, my Lord, for all that I'm worth;
   . . .

4) Gonna die, my Lord, for all that I'm worth;
   . . .

5) Gonna live, my Lord, for all that I'm worth;
   . . .

6) Gonna sing, my Lord, for all that I'm worth;
   . . .

# 11. Hear, O Lord

RAY REPP

Chorus:    Hear, O Lord, the sound of my call;
                Hear, O Lord, and have mercy.
                My soul is longing for the glory of you.
                O hear, O Lord, and answer me.

1)    Ev'ry night before I sleep
      I pray my soul to take,
      Or else I pray that loneliness
      Is gone when I awake.

2)    Why do I no longer feel
      Like I've a place to stay?
      O take me where someone will care,
      So fear will go away.

3)    In you, O Lord, I place my cares
      And all my troubles too.
      O grant, dear Lord, that some day soon
      I'll live in peace with you.

## 12. Here We Are

RAY REPP

Chorus: Here we are all together
    As we sing our song joyfully.
    Here we are joined together
    As we pray we'll always be.

1) Join we now as friends, and celebrate the
  Brotherhood we share all as one.
  Keep the fire burning, kindle it with care,
  And we'll all join in and sing.

2) Freedom we do shout for ev'ry body,
  And, unless there is, we should pray that
  Soon there will be one true brotherhood;
  Let us all join in and sing.

3) Glorify the Lord with all our voices
  Show him we're sincere by all our deeds.
  Shout the joys of freedom ev'rywhere,
  And we'll all join in and sing.

4) Happy is the man who does his best to
  Free the troubled world from all its pain.
  Join we with that man and free the world,
  As we all join in and sing.

5) Let us make the world an Alleluia!
  Let us make the world a better place.
  Keep a smile handy, have a helping hand;
  Let us all join in and sing.

# 13. I Am the Way

MICHAEL WYNNE

Chorus:   I am the Way, I am the Truth,
I am the Light and the Life.
Come, I invite you to come follow me,
And be blessed and refreshed and made one in my
love.

1)   Hear, all of you who do not have a dream
That you reach out to hold;
Come, let me show you a dream which is right by your
side

If you'll just look around.
Come be blessed and refreshed and made one in my love.

2)   Hear, all of you who are lost in the crowd
And who search for yourselves.
Come, won't you listen while I show the strength and the
power

And life that you hold?
Come be blessed and refreshed and made one in my love.

3)   Hear all of you who must live without joy
Or who suffer alone;
Come, I will teach all I've learned from my cross and my
tears

And my life among you.
Come be blessed and refreshed and made one in my love.

4)   Hear all of you who are bored and don't listen
Because you don't care.
Come let me show you that this is the sin that is keeping
Mankind from my joy.
Come be blessed and refreshed and made one in my love.

5) Hear, all of you who have chosen to follow
The road that I walk.
Come, in my word and my bread you will find what you
need
To walk faithful and strong.
Come be blessed and refreshed and made one in my love.


## 14. I'm Ready to Follow

J. H. MIFFLETON

Chorus: I'm ready to follow
Walking on with joy now;
The Master calls,
"Won't you be one, be one with me?"

1) Oh, let us thank the Lord our God
For this sacrifice to set us free;
He gave his life.

2) Oh, let us thank the Lord our God
For this gift of love: he's with us now,
The Lord above.

3) Oh, let us thank the Lord our God
For one and all he gives us life,
The great and small.

4) Oh, let us thank the Lord our God
For this our land, he made it all;
It was his plan.

# 15. Let Us Break Bread Together

ROBERT BLUE

1) Let us break bread together at the altar,
   Break bread together we are one;
   For when we are together
   Christ is with us,
   Break bread together for we are one.

2) Let us drink wine together at the altar,
   Drink wine together we are one;
   For when we are together
   Christ is with us,
   Drink wine together for we are one.

3) Let us offer together gifts at the altar,
   Offer together we are one;
   For when we are together
   Christ is with us,
   Offer together for we are one.

4) Let us join hands together at the altar,
   Join hands together we are one;
   For when we are together
   Christ is with us,
   Join hands together for we are one.

5) Let us love one another at the altar,
   Love one another we are one;
   For when we are together
   Christ is with us,
   Love one another for we are one.

# 16. Of My Hands

RAY REPP

Chorus:    Of my hands I give to you, O Lord,
            Of my hands I give to you.
            I give to you as you gave to me;
            Of my hands I give to you.

            Of my heart I give to you, O Lord,
            . . .

1)    You let us out of darkness when we knew not where to go.
     You asked us then to follow you, and we said "No."

            Of my life I give to you, O Lord,
            . . .

            Of my self I give to you, O Lord,
            . . .

2)    You suffered for the sake of man that we might live with
     you.
     O may we show our gratefulness in what we say and do.

            Of my hands I give to you, O Lord,
            . . .

# 17. Shout From the Highest Mountain

RAY REPP

Chorus:    Shout from the highest mountain
The glory of the Lord;
Let all men rejoice in him.
Sing from the highest mountain
The praises of the Lord;
Let all men know the wonders of our God!

1)    For all the good things the Lord has done for us
Let us join now in song.

2)    For all the birds in the trees and the sky
And all nature as well.

3)    For all the children who play in the fields:
May they always be young.

4)    For all the people who follow his way,
Those who bring joy to men.

5)    And for our country that keeps us in peace:
May we always be free.

## 18. Sing Praise to the Lord

JOSEPH WISE

Chorus:    Sing praise to the Lord, Alleluia.
             Sing praise to the Lord, Alleluia.
             Sing praise to the Lord, Alleluia.
             Sing, sing to my Lord.

1)    His word is searing deep in my soul,
       It lights, it fires, it pains.
       He pleads for all that's closed up within,
       And all my great heart could give, and all my great heart
           could give.

2)    He tells me joy is being with him,
       Being nailed is to be free.
       His weary arms reach out for my love:
       When will I answer His call, when will I answer His call?

3)    Wounded, frightened, love-poor do I come
       And longing to be free.
       His loving hand is tender and strong;
       He touches all that I am, He touches all that I am.

4)    The bread He gives is none but Himself,
       His body, blood and life.
       He give me all my brothers to love
       In life that here just begins, in life that here just begins.

5)    In Jesus God has given His love,
       His mercy has been shown,
       And in our love we shout out to all:
       Yes, Jesus is our true love, yes, Jesus is our true love.

# 19. Sons of God

JAMES THIEM

Chorus:  Sons of God, hear his holy Word!
Gather 'round the table of the Lord!
Eat his Body, drink his Blood,
And we'll sing a song of love:
Allelu, allelu, allelu, alleluia!

1)  Brothers, sisters, we are one,
And our life has just begun;
In the Spirit we are young;
We can live forever.

2)  Shout together to the Lord
Who has promised our reward:
Happiness a hundred fold,
And we'll live forever.

3)  Jesus gave a new command
That we love our fellow man
Till we reach the promised land,
Where we'll live forever.

4)  If we want to live with him,
We must also die with him,
Die to selfishness and sin,
And we'll rise forever.

5)  Make the world a unity,
Make all men one family
Till we meet the Trinity
And live with them forever.

6)  With the Church we celebrate,
Jesus' coming we await;
So we make a holiday,
So we'll live forever.

## 20. Take Our Bread

JOSEPH WISE

Chorus:    Take our bread we ask you.
Take our hearts, we love you.
Take our lives, O Father,
We are yours, we are yours.

1)    Yours as we stand at the table you set;
Yours as we eat the bread our hearts can't forget.
We are the sign of your life with us yet,
We are yours, we are yours.

2)    Your holy people standing washed in your blood,
Spirit filled yet hungry we await your food.
We are poor, but we've brought ourselves, the best we could;
We are yours, we are yours.

# 21. There Are But Three Things That Last

J. H. MIFFLETON

Chorus:    There are but three things that last,
Faith, Hope, Faith, Hope and Love,
But the greatest of these is Love.

1)   If my voice were like an angel's,
If the future were mine,
I have nothing at all without Love, without Love.

2)   If my mind could hold God's secret's,
Move great mountains with faith,
I have nothing at all without Love, without Love.

3)   If I bought the world tomorrow,
Lay my life down today,
I have nothing at all without Love, without Love.

4)   Love is patient, it's creative,
Meek, it's shy when it's praised;
I have nothing at all without Love, without Love.

5)   Love makes friends because it's selfless,
Glad when good men succeed;
I have nothing at all without Love, without Love.

6)   Love has endless, endless mercy,
Everlasting its trust;
I have nothing at all without Love, without Love.

# 22. There Is None Like Him

CLARENCE RIVERS

Chorus:    Holy, holy Lord!
            Holy is the Lord of Hosts!

1)    He is greater than the universe,
        The world could not contain him.
        Yet he dwells within our hearts,
        O there is none like him.

2)    He did not ever need us,
        Yet he made us out of love,
        And he wants us to be with him.
        O there is none like him.

3)    He was born of a virgin,
        And he lived as a common man,
        Yet none the less our God
        O there is none like him.

4)    He was the God immortal,
        Yet he died upon a cross,
        And in dying he slew death.
        O there is none like him.

5)    He was the God almighty,
        Yet he did not use his power,
        And his weakness was like strength.
        O there is none like him.

6)    He lived with us, he died for us,
        He made himself our food.
        We are members of his Body.
        O there is none like him.

# 23. They'll Know We Are Christians by Our Love

PETER SCHOLTES

Chorus: And they'll know we are Christians
    By our love, by our love;
    Yes, they'll know we are Christians by our love.

1) We are one in the Spirit,
  We are one in the Lord,
  We are one in the Spirit,
  We are one in the Lord,
  And we pray that all unity may one day be restored.

2) We will walk with each other,
  We will walk hand in hand,
  We will walk with each other,
  We will walk hand in hand,
  And together we'll spread the news that God is in our land.

3) We will work with each other,
  We will work side by side,
  We will work with each other,
  We will work side by side,
  And we'll guard each man's dignity and save each man's
    pride.

4) All praise to the Father,
  From whom all things come,
  And all praise to Christ Jesus,
  His only Son,
  And all praise to the Spirit, who makes us one.

## 24. We Are Your Bread

JOSEPH WISE

Chorus:    We are your bread now; he is our life now.
We are your bread now; the bread of love are we.
We are your heart now; we are your flesh now.
We are your bread now; the bread of love are we.

1) With one heart and one voice we sing to him we know.
In the breaking of the bread of our table and ourselves,
A song of love with hearts full open and full free,
In the word of him who melodies our lives.

2) How to sing the joy we know just standing here in you,
On this the day of our dying and our birth;
Or the wonder that we feel to know that this, the bread of
heav'n,
Was first and is still the bread of earth.

3) Alleluia, alleluia, alleluia, my Lord,
Alleluia, alleluia, there is no word to sing,
Only a word to live, the love word of God.
The rainbow thanks the word of self we bring.

4) Give us this day, our Lord, our daily bread;
The bread of all we do and all this day we are to meet.
Take us with trust to every table that you set,
That we never be afraid to take and eat.

## 25. We Shall Overcome

1) We shall overcome,
   We shall overcome,
   We shall overcome some day.
   Oh, deep in my heart,
   I do believe
   That we shall overcome some day.

2) We shall live in peace,
   . . .

3) The truth will make us free,
   . . .

4) We are not afraid,
   . . .

5) We shall overcome,
   . . .

# 26. What a Great Thing It Is

RAY REPP

Chorus:　　What a great thing it is,
　　　　　　　　　(What a great thing it is)
　　　　　　And oh, how pleasant it can be,
　　　　　　　　　(Oh how pleasant it can be)
　　　　　　For all God's people to live together in peace.

　　　　　　So now tell ev'ryone you meet
　　　　　　　　　(Now tell ev'ryone you meet)
　　　　　　The joy that we were meant to see
　　　　　　　　　(Joy that we were meant to see)
　　　　　　When all God's people live together in peace.

1)　　The Lord gave ev'ryone a law that we should
　　　　Love and follow ev'ry call from him.

2)　　The Father promised us a home where we could
　　　　Live together as a family.

3)　　Brothers, sisters are we all because we're
　　　　Made as equal in the sight of God.

4)　　All you children of the Lord sing out and
　　　　Praise our God for all eternity.

## 27. You Are My People

SISTER GERMAINE

Chorus:    You are my people,
                I am your God.
                You are my people,
                Close to my heart.

1)     Lord, we are thirsty, walkin' through this desert land!
       Lord, we are thirsty, give us to drink!
       The Lord sent water from the rock
       To give his people to drink.

2)     Lord, we are hungry, walkin' through this desert land!
       Lord, we are hungry, give us some food!
       The Lord sent manna from the sky
       To give his people food.

3)     Lord, we are weary, lost in this desert land!
       Lord, we are weary, show us the way!
       The Lord sent a pillar of cloud by day, a pillar of fire
                                by night,

       To show his people the way.

4)     Still they cried out, and they complained:
       "Where is the Savior, the anointed one?"
       The Lord sent his only Son,
       Christ, the anointed one.

5)     I give you my body to be your food;
       My blood I pour out that you may never thirst.
       I give you my light; I give you my love;
       I give you my Spirit of love.